W O O D S
w o r o k s
WITH BLIZZARD

WOODWORKs

WITH BLIZZARD

RICHARD BLIZZARD

BBC Books

ACKNOWLEDGEMENTS

Making the furniture for a book and the many different pieces and half-made pieces needed for a television series always needs a vast amount of work and the assistance of some very skilled people. This book and series were different from any previous series, however, in that many companies were prepared to help me by sponsoring the making of the prototypes for the projects. Therefore a special 'thank you' is due to:

Makita Electric (UK) Ltd, in particular George Yamamoto, Derrick Marshall, Terry Bicker, Roger Broomhall, Carol Chant and Chris Bull

AEG, in particular Herbert Klostermann, Jim Murray, Norman Collier and Mike Lustig

Stanley Tools, in particular David Prosser, John Spon-Smith and Geoff Baldwin (who kept an eye on us!)

Finnish Swedish Timber Council, in particular Peter Grimsdale, Jack Baird, Sharron Clay and Hilary Grimsdale

Kronospan Ltd, in particular Jim Hay and Nigel Barber

Medite of Europe Ltd, in particular G T A Rhodes and Malcolm Cowley

Record Marples Ltd, in particular Roger Cottle

European Industrial Services Ltd (Nettlefolds screws), in particular Bob Smith, Sue Sidhu and Janet Webber

Sadolin (UK) Ltd, in particular Mark Robbins

Woodworking Machines of Switzerland, in particular Bruce Pollard

Emmerich (Berlon) Ltd, in particular Bill Emmerich

Cuprinol Ltd

Mr Jamiesons (Aberdeen) Ltd

At the BBC, thanks are due to Chris Stone at Bristol and Janet Brookes at Birmingham for sorting out all the contract details, and also to Debbie Hood; to Bernie Cavender who designed this book and helped carry summer houses; and to Jennie Allen whose encouragement and editing skills will contribute to the book's success.

Finally, thank you to Peter Farley and Mervyn Hurford for all the working drawings (late nights and rushes!), and also to Jenny Spring and Mary Davis who typed the scripts.

The plans for the projects were drawn by Peter Farley, Mervyn Hurford and Stephanie Banks

The black and white and colour photographs were taken by Peter Pugh-Cook except those on page 74 (bottom left and right) which were supplied by AEG (UK) Ltd

The diagrams in the tools and techniques section were drawn by Alan Burton

The publishers would like to thank Stanley Tools, Makita Electric (UK) Ltd and AEG (UK) Ltd for their assistance.

Published by BBC Books,
A division of BBC Enterprises Ltd
Woodlands, 80 Wood Lane, London W12 0TT
First published 1989
© Richard Blizzard 1989

ISBN 0 563 20802 3

Typeset in 10 on 11 point Gill
by Rowland Phototypesetting Ltd,
Bury St Edmunds, Suffolk
Colour separations by Dot Gradations Ltd
Printed and bound in Great Britain by
Redwood Burn Ltd, Trowbridge, Wiltshire
Jacket/cover printed by Belmont Press,
Northampton

CONTENTS

Throughout the book metric measurements are given first, followed by imperial measurements in brackets

FOREWORD

By
Peter Grimsdale
Director of the Swedish Finnish
Timber Council

Where would we be without timber? Whether you are an ardent DIY'er or not, just look around your home and you'll realise that, despite the advent of synthetic materials we are still dependent upon this most natural, attractive and practical of Nature's raw materials.

In recent years much has been written about the disappearing forests of the world. Unfortunately, in the case of some tropical rain forests this is true, and there has to be great concern about the effect of this depletion on our environment and the future supply of exotic tropical hardwoods which come from these forests. But fortunately for timber lovers, there is a solution to this problem. We can control the planting and felling of our forests, and for some two centuries Sweden and Finland have been doing just that. There are strict rules in these countries which ensure that the annual growth is always greater than the usage. For these reasons there is more timber in the Scandinavian forests today than at any time in history. Every hour of every day there is sufficient growth to provide trees for at least 250 houses constructed wholly of timber. There are enough mature trees for every man, woman and child in the world to have 400 each!

Scandinavian softwoods represent about one half of all the timber consumed in the UK and over 80% of that used by DIY'ers. Therefore, it is readily available at almost every timber merchant and DIY outlet. Knowing Richard Blizzard as I do, it is not surprising to me that he has taken note of all these factors in the preparation of the projects for this book, the majority of which are made from renewable softwoods.

I am delighted to be given this opportunity of opening the latest Richard Blizzard book. I know that you will derive great pleasure from working with timber under Richard's expert guidance, and your pride in the finished product will be heightened by the knowledge that the raw material is being assured for future generations by the care and expertise of softwood foresters.

SPICE RACK

In most homes there never seems to be enough shelf space. This small unit provides ideal storage for spice jars in the kitchen and, by simply altering the dimensions, is easy to adapt to other places and uses around the home.

Free-standing or suitable for hanging on the wall, the basic construction of the unit is simple but very strong. The joint used is a traditional through housing joint (see page 99). Wooden bars on the front prevent things falling off, although these could be left off or reduced in width to suit your own requirements. Nordic Redwood is used throughout. Ask your timber merchant if he has any 'short ends' that are suitable for this job – you'll be doing each other a favour. I like to leave 'fresh' timber in my workshop for at least a couple of weeks before starting work on it.

1 Make a start by studying the plans. You'll see that the only joint used is a through housing joint. The top and bottom boards fit into slots cut in the uprights.

2 Cut all 4 shelves to length and, with a very sharp smoothing plane, work over them until they are perfectly smooth. When you have finished, the shelves should be ready to fit and you can use them to mark out the width of the housing joints on the uprights. If you use the shelves as a measure before you plane them, you will find that after you have done so they will fit too loosely in the housing joints.

3 Cut out the 2 uprights and clamp them together. Use the ends of the shelves to help you pencil in the width of the 4 housing joints on the sides of the uprights, measuring carefully the distance between each one. Then separate the uprights and again use the shelf to pencil in the full length of the housings across each upright. Go over all your lines with a marking knife and gauge as explained on page 99.

4 Cut out the housing joints using either a tenon saw, chisel and hand router, or an electric router, as explained on page 99.

5 Now cut the slots in the uprights into which the decorative top and bottom cross members will fit. (If you want the unit to be free-standing then you only need the top one.) Mark out the slots at top and bottom (if appropriate) of the uprights and use a tenon saw (see page 99) to cut down the sides of the slot and a coping saw (see page 101) to cut across the bottom. You may then need to use a chisel to tidy up the corners.

Finally chamfer off the front corners of the uprights using a coping saw and spokeshave (see page 105).

6 Mark and cut out the top and bottom cross members using a spokeshave to help you achieve the attractive gentle curves.

7 Pre-drill holes in both ends of the cross members and in the back edges of the 2 uprights so that you can eventually screw this 'framework' together as well as glue it. This is particularly important if you are going to hang the unit on the wall as the frame then has to take the full weight of the objects on the shelves.

8 Mark, cut out and shape the front lips for the shelves. Use a coping saw to cut the rounded edges out roughly, then a spokeshave to smooth them off.

9 Now you are ready to assemble and glue the unit.
i Assemble the uprights, cross members and shelves dry to check that everything fits snugly. Use glasspaper to correct any problem areas and a very sharp smoothing plane to remove any pencil marks.
ii Have your sash cramps (see page 103) and pieces of waste wood ready for the actual glueing operation. I always find it a good idea to set the cramps to the correct width at this stage – it saves a lot of hurried fumbling later.
iii Apply glue to the housing joints first and cramp the shelves in place. Check that the unit is square by laying a batten diagonally from corner to corner. Mark the corners off in pencil and lay the batten across the other diagonal. If the pencil marks don't line up with these corners, slacken off the cramps and, using a piece of waste wood and a hammer, firmly tap all the joints to tighten them up. Re-set all the cramps and check the diagonals again. Once the unit is square, glue the top and (if using) bottom cross members into the slots in the uprights. Allow 24 hours for the glue to 'cure' (dry).
iv When the glue has cured completely, remove the cramps and use a sharp smoothing plane to remove any traces of glue that may have oozed out of the joints. Then glue the front lips onto the shelves.

10 Finally you should drive screws into the top and bottom cross members from the back of the uprights via the pre-drilled holes to increase the strength of the framework.

To hang the unit on the wall, drive screws through the top and bottom cross members.

11 If you intend to use the shelves in the kitchen or bathroom you may wish to give them several coats of polyurethane varnish to protect them from stains. Otherwise several layers of furniture polish will be enough to protect and enhance this useful storage unit.

Cutting list

Uprights	2 off	806 × 146 × 22mm (31¾ × 5¾ × ⅞in)	Timber
Shelves	4 off	505 × 146 × 22mm (19⅞ × 5¾ × ⅞in)	Timber
Shelving front lip	3 off	560 × 47 × 16mm (22 × 1⅞ × ⅝in)	Timber
Rear cross members	2 off	603 × 133 × 22mm (23¾ × 5¼ × ⅞in)	Timber

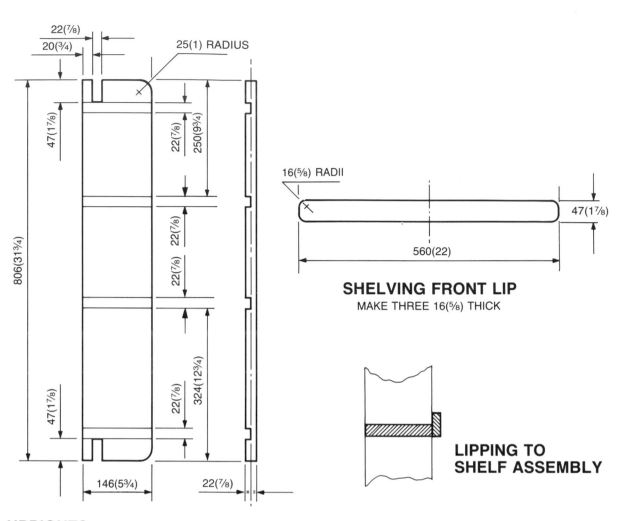

22(⅞)
20(¾)
25(1) RADIUS
47(1⅞)
22(⅞)
250(9¾)
22(⅞)
22(⅞)
22(⅞)
324(12¾)
806(31¾)
47(1⅞)
146(5¾)
22(⅞)

UPRIGHTS MAKE TWO ONE OF EACH HAND

16(⅝) RADII
47(1⅞)
560(22)

SHELVING FRONT LIP
MAKE THREE 16(⅝) THICK

LIPPING TO SHELF ASSEMBLY

SHELVES
MAKE FOUR 505 × 146 × 22(19⅞ × 5¾ × ⅞)

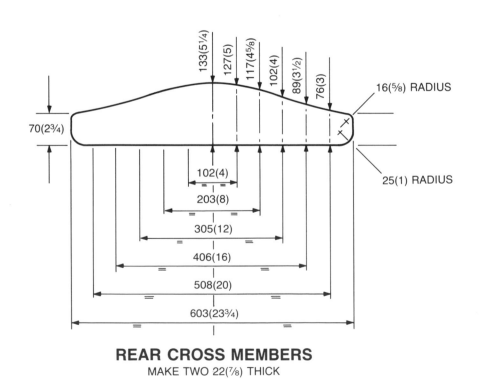

133(5¼)
127(5)
117(4⅝)
102(4)
89(3½)
76(3)
16(⅝) RADIUS
70(2¾)
25(1) RADIUS
102(4)
203(8)
305(12)
406(16)
508(20)
603(23¾)

REAR CROSS MEMBERS
MAKE TWO 22(⅞) THICK

SCREEN

Screens were first used to break the cold draughts that swept through castles and large houses. In later days it became fashionable to use small fire screens to prevent the heat from damaging the complexions of the ladies who seated themselves in front of blazing hearths. In addition to screens designed to break the cold winds that howled through, carpenters devised seating with tall wood backs to stop draughts. These settles are now prized possessions, although with the introduction of central heating and double glazing, they no longer fulfil the function for which they were originally designed.

However, modern man has re-discovered something that his ancestors knew well: natural materials are the best things with which to decorate any house. Wooden panelled walls will always look good and improve with age. Today many houses use pine wall panelling, which takes on a deep rich mellow colour as it ages.

And so to the modern screen, which can be 'dressed' in a variety of fabrics, even silk. An attractive screen, carefully lit using natural or artificial light, will add a new dimension to your room. They make effective room dividers in open-plan houses and can also be used to hide awkward corners or eyesores that you can't get rid of.

This screen is a good project for a beginner as only one type of joint has to be cut – a through mortice and tenon; all the rest of the construction is glued. The three panels are identical, so if you intend to build all three, mark them out together. This saves time and will be more accurate. The timber used is Nordic Redwood. The horizontal battens were roofing battens bought from a builders' merchant. There are several different sizes and qualities of batten. I searched through a big pile to select mine, which were very clean, straight and almost knot-free. If you cannot find something similar you will need to find someone with a circular saw to cut the battens up for you, but this is quite a lot of extra work.

1 Having selected your timber for the 6 verticals and 6 rails for your 3 panels, mark on in pencil the face side and face edge (see page 99).

Clamp the rails together and pencil in the shoulder lines for your through mortice and tenon joints (see page 101). Separate the pieces and continue the shoulder lines all round each rail, then 'knife in' all the pencil lines with a marking knife.

2 Now follow the general instructions on page 101 for setting your mortice gauge and marking off all the tenons on the rails and mortice slots on the verticals. When you are sure you have marked everything correctly (it is a good idea to scribble over the waste pieces in pencil), cut the joints, again following the instructions on page 101.

3 Fit all the joints together 'dry' and use a long batten diagonally from corner to corner of each panel to check for squareness (see page 23, step 6). Use a sharp smoothing plane to clean up all the timber and then glue and cramp the 3 frameworks together.

4 Now cut to length and plane the 2 outer and 1 central vertical battens and the 2 horizontal battens for the interior of each panel. These form a sort of rebate into which the horizontal slats are fixed.

Glue the outer vertical battens into position first, making absolutely certain that they are fitted exactly in the centre of the main uprights. Do the same for the horizontal battens at top and bottom. Finally glue on the central vertical batten. Leave for 24 hours for the glue to 'cure'.

5 Select and cut to length all the horizontal slats for each panel and plane them smooth. Be careful to cut these accurately so that they fit comfortably between the uprights. Measure and mark the position for each slat on the interior vertical battens of each panel. Note from the plans that they are placed across alternately on either side of the framework. Check all your measurements once again and then glue the slats into place.

6 If you intend to dress the screen

with a light fabric it is particularly important to ensure that the wood has been planed as smooth as possible. So use a smoothing plane on the outside of the framework, and glasspaper wrapped round a cork block or a palm sander (see page 105) on the inside edges. This latter tool has the advantage of being able to get right into the 90° corners of the screen.

7 The 3 panels are held together by hinges. Use traditional brass hinges for this. You will need to cut shallow rebates on the framework to accommodate them, and for this you will need a marking gauge, which is similar to a mortice gauge, except that it has 1 spike, not 2 (see page 99).

Clamp 2 of the panels together and pencil in the length of the hinge flaps in the appropriate places at top and bottom of the side of each framework. Lay the hinges in position. Set the gauge fence on the edge of the flap and adjust the spike until it touches the central pin in the hinge. Transfer this width onto the edge of each framework using the spike to score the line. This first marking is to accommodate the hinge width. Now separate the panels and re-set the gauge to the thickness of the flap and transfer this marking onto the sides of the frames. The spike on the gauge leaves a perfect line for the chisel to fit into.

Before chiselling out these areas to take the hinge flaps, I always work around them with a large chisel, cutting in just a little more deeply than the gauge spike can. This is particularly useful on the cross grain; otherwise there is a tendency for the groove to 'tear back' on either side of the rebate. Then, working carefully with a large chisel, lightly chip out the wood. Finish off with the chisel held in both hands for the final shaving of wood.

Now repeat the whole operation with the third panel and the other edge of the middle panel. Think carefully about the positioning of the second set of hinges on the middle framework as they must be placed so that the 3 panels will fold up flat. Look at the plans on page 16 and get someone to help you practise folding them up before you make any cuts.

When you have cut all the rebates you can screw the hinges in place. It is very important that the screw heads lie flush with the hinge flaps – otherwise the hinge will 'bind' when the screen is folded, so be sure to use screws that fit exactly in the countersunk hinge holes.

10 I used matt polyurethane varnish to finish off the panels using a piece of lint-free cloth to rub the polyurethane into the wood. Remember that there are dozens of 90° angles in this framework and it is important not to get a build-up of varnish in these corners as this will lead to globules of varnish running down the cross battens which look very ugly.

Once the varnish is dry, use glasspaper to 'cutback' the wood grain that will have been raised when applying the varnish and then apply a second coat.

Cutting list

Main frame	verticals	6 off	1830 × 44 × 28mm (72 × 1¾ × 1⅛in)	Timber
	horizontal rails	6 off	610 × 44 × 28mm (24 × 1¾ × 1⅛in)	Timber
Battens	outer	6 off	1774 × 20 × 20mm (69¾ × ¾ × ¾in)	Timber
	central	3 off	1734 × 20 × 20mm (68¼ × ¾ × ¾in)	Timber
	horizontal	6 off	514 × 20 × 20mm (20¼ × ¾ × ¾in)	Timber
Slats		33 off	554 × 20 × 12mm (21¾ × ¾ × ½in)	Timber

Ancillaries

	6 off	76mm (3in) brass hinges

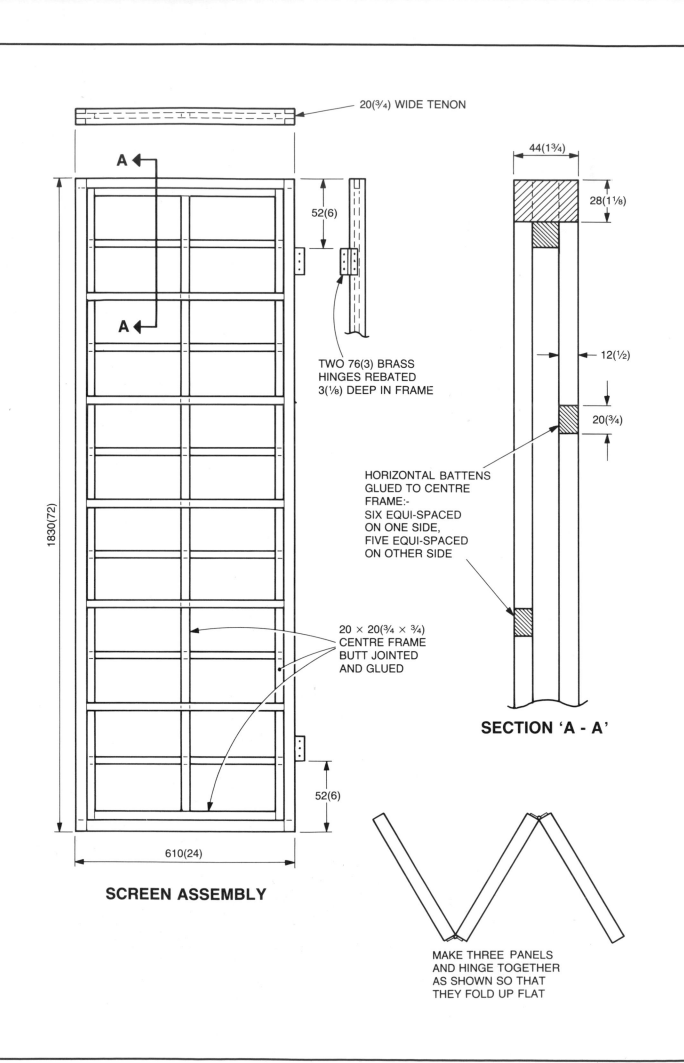

20(¾) WIDE TENON

52(6)

TWO 76(3) BRASS
HINGES REBATED
3(⅛) DEEP IN FRAME

44(1¾)

28(1⅛)

12(½)

20(¾)

HORIZONTAL BATTENS
GLUED TO CENTRE
FRAME:-
SIX EQUI-SPACED
ON ONE SIDE,
FIVE EQUI-SPACED
ON OTHER SIDE

SECTION 'A - A'

1830(72)

20 × 20(¾ × ¾)
CENTRE FRAME
BUTT JOINTED
AND GLUED

52(6)

610(24)

SCREEN ASSEMBLY

MAKE THREE PANELS
AND HINGE TOGETHER
AS SHOWN SO THAT
THEY FOLD UP FLAT

Spice rack

Finishing the screen using an electric palm sander

TEAK BLANKET CHEST

The traditional pine blanket chest on page 45 is a wonderful project for those with time and intermediate carpentry skills. However, if you're looking for a simpler and speedier answer to your storage problems this version may be the answer. A visit to your local DIY superstore will show you the ever-growing range of man-made boards from which to choose the ideal colour for your home plus the range of devices that you can use to fit them together. I have chosen teak veneer but plain white and textured black ash are also very popular.

If you want to make life really simple for yourself choose a board that is already cut and finished to the sizes you want (the measurements in the cutting list are fairly standard). This saves the bother of ironing on a veneer strip round the edges of the sides and lid.

If you can measure, cut and drill holes accurately you will have no problems building this chest and the end product will give you a real sense of achievement. The only procedure you need to worry about is cutting the man-made board without chipping the veneer. I suggest you use a jigsaw fitted with a metal-cutting blade or an electric saw fitted with a tungsten carbide blade (see page 98) and experiment on offcuts before tackling the chest itself.

Finally, I would recommend using Multis (see page 104) to screw the boards together. These are a new type of screw particularly suited to use on man-made boards and they come in a range of colours to match the finish you choose.

1 Study the cutting list before you go to the DIY store. It will save both time and aggravation later. The chest is made from a total of nine pieces (excluding the moulding strips): 2 ends; 2 sides; 1 base; 2 plinth pieces; 1 centre strip to support the base; and 1 lid.

2 First cut the 2 ends to length, if necessary, and use a pencil to mark the position of the base and the 2 plinth pieces. The easiest and most accurate way to do this is to lay a piece of the same board onto the ends, and use this as a guide to pencil round.

Once this is done, measure out carefully where all the screws will go. It is very useful to have a countersink bit for your drill for all the holes that must now be drilled (see page 104). Don't forget that the countersink must not be too deep – just enough to take the head of the screw. If you countersink too deeply, the chipboard underneath will show around the screw head. Practise drilling and countersinking on a waste piece in order to get this right. If you have a drill stand, it will have a stop on it to prevent you from drilling too deep once you have set it to the correct drilling depth.

Bore all the screw holes required in the ends.

3 Now cut the 2 plinths to length and screw these to the 2 ends.

4 Measure and cut the base piece to length and lay it in position. Drive screws from the top of the base into the plinth pieces and from the outside of the ends into the ends of the base.

5 To 'firm up' the plinth and give added support to the base, fit a centre piece from back to front across the underneath of the base. Screw it in position via the top of the base and the outside of the plinths.

6 Now you are ready to fit the sides. You will see from the drawings that these are not quite as high as the 2 ends. This is done to allow blankets in the chest to 'breathe' and to allow for the piano hinge which attaches the lid to the chest to be recessed. Cut the sides to length and screw them in position via the outside of the ends.

7 Now you need to iron veneer strips onto any exposed cut edges of the chest. (See page 32, step 13 for instructions.) Once the glue has dried or 'cured' (usually about 10 minutes) trim off any excess.

8 I decorated the chest with mouldings. Builders' merchants keep many different types of mouldings, but if you have an electric router (see page 98) you can make your own using a moulding cutter.

One word of advice. Don't try to rout a moulding on a very thin piece of wood. Buy a piece of thicker timber, run the router along the edge and then cut off the moulding to the width you require. With this method the wood is easy to hold in the vice while it is worked on with the router. This really is the simplest and safest method.

The diamond shape on the front was made by cutting the shape out of board and glueing moulding round the edges.

Use a mitre block and tenon saw to cut all the 45° angles on the ends of the mouldings (see page 102). All the mouldings were treated with 2 coats of mahogany wood stain to give the attractive contrast you can see in the photograph on page 35. Attach the mouldings to the chest with screws that you should drive into the wood from the inside of the chest, making sure they do not break through.

As a final piece of decoration I added brass handles to the sides.

9 Cut the lid to length and iron on veneer strips as necessary. Screw a length of piano hinge (available from ironmongers) along one edge. Then screw the other side of the hinge to the chest. Once this is done, screw a brass cabinet stay to the inside of the chest and the lid to prevent the lid from falling backwards and pulling the hinge out.

10 It is possible that, despite your best efforts, there may be one or two places where the chipboard shows through chips in the veneer. You can buy wax furniture sticks of different colours that are ideal for these tiny touch-up jobs. Rub wax on the chip or crack, polish with a soft cloth and it will hide the mark completely.

Cutting list

Side	2 off	1067 × 387 × 14mm (42 × 15¼ × ⁹⁄₁₆in)	Chipboard
End	2 off	508 × 508 × 14mm (20 × 20 × ⁹⁄₁₆in)	Chipboard
Base	1 off	1067 × 508 × 14mm (42 × 20 × ⁹⁄₁₆in)	Chipboard
Plinth	2 off	1067 × 102 × 14mm (42 × 4 × ⁹⁄₁₆in)	Chipboard
Centre support	1 off	430 × 102 × 14mm (16⅞ × 4 × ⁹⁄₁₆in)	Chipboard
Lid	1 off	1168 × 559 × 14mm (46 × 22 × ⁹⁄₁₆in)	Chipboard
Decorative diamond	1 off	406 × 165 × 20mm (16 × 6½ × ¾in)	Timber
Decorative moulding	4 off	1165 × 35 × 12mm (45⅞ × 1⅜ × ½in)	Timber
	4 off	578 × 35 × 12mm (22¾ × 1⅜ × ½in)	Timber

Ancillaries

	1 off	1067mm (42in) × 12mm (½in) piano hinge
	1 off	203mm (8in) brass cabinet stay
	4 off	Decorative brass handles

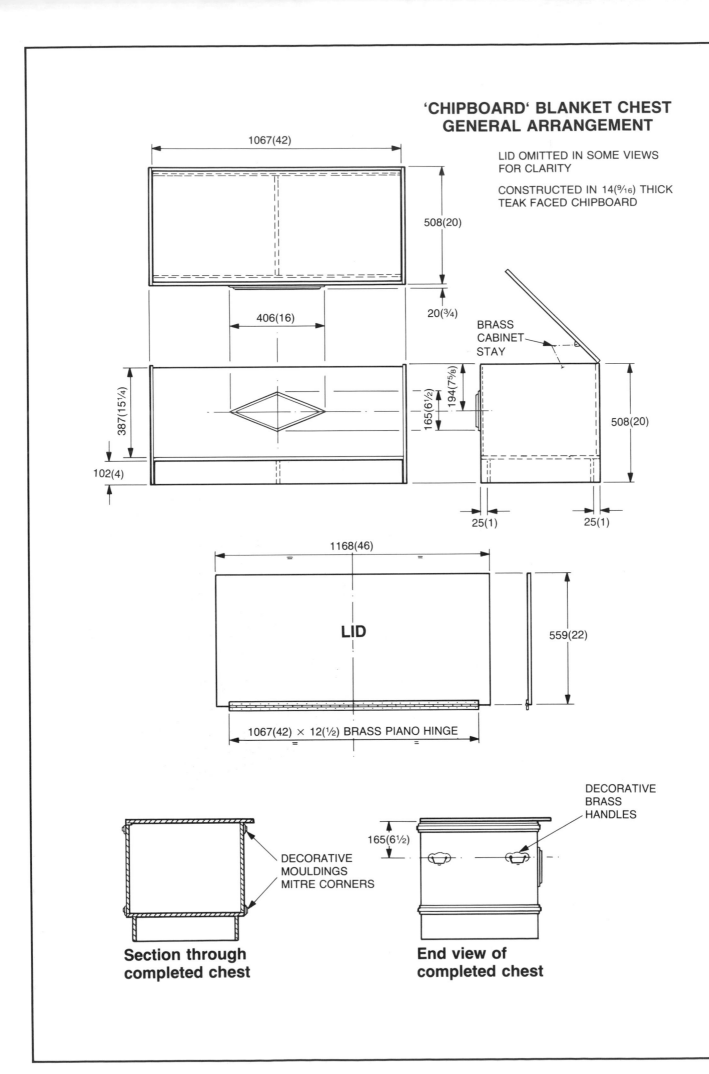

'CHIPBOARD' BLANKET CHEST
GENERAL ARRANGEMENT

LID OMITTED IN SOME VIEWS
FOR CLARITY

CONSTRUCTED IN 14(9/16) THICK
TEAK FACED CHIPBOARD

1067(42)

508(20)

20(¾)

406(16)

387(15¼)

102(4)

165(6½)

194(7⅝)

BRASS
CABINET
STAY

508(20)

25(1)   25(1)

1168(46)

LID

559(22)

1067(42) × 12(½) BRASS PIANO HINGE

DECORATIVE
BRASS
HANDLES

DECORATIVE
MOULDINGS
MITRE CORNERS

165(6½)

**Section through
completed chest**

**End view of
completed chest**

WELSH DRESSER

This is a very practical piece of furniture made in Nordic pine. As well as providing useful shelf space for plates or books, it has the added optional feature of a folding book shelf on which to support a cookery book out of harm's way of the ingredients. The tongue-and-groove panelling used for the back adds to the traditional look of this classic dresser top.

The techniques used are stopped housing joints and a single mortice and tenon. So if you have already made the simple spice rack on page 9 you will find this will be a natural extension of your carpentry skills.

1   The first job is to make the 2 upright end panels. As you are now embarked on a piece of high-class cabinet-making you need to cut stopped housing joints in these (see page 99) so that the ends of the shelves will be concealed.

Cut the end panels to length and pencil in the curved shaping but do not cut away the waste wood yet. Pencil in the position of the housing joints for the 2 shelves (using your shelving timber as a width guide) and the top front cross member. Pencil in too the large rebate that will hold the back panelling flush with the ends.

Now cut the housing joints. Remember that these are *stopped* housing joints and that the technique for cutting these using hand tools is different from cutting through joints. Follow the advice on page 99 and make sure that you are working with good sharp chisels. Of course, if you have an electric router (see page 98) all that is necessary is to set a piece of batten in place as a fence, fit the appropriate width cutter and away you go. Electric tools like this make you realise with a sense of wonder the skills of a bygone age when everything had to be done through sheer physical hand labour.

2   Once you have cut the housing joints you need to cut the rebates along the back edges of the end panels. It is best to buy your panelling for the back before you cut this to make sure you have pencilled in the depth correctly. Use a rebate plane or an electric router to cut the rebates (see page 98).

3   Cut the 2 shelves to length, then cut away the notch at each of the front corners which will allow the ends to fit into the stopped housing joints. When these are assembled into the end panels, the backs of the shelves will lie flush with the bottom of the rebate, allowing the panelling to butt up against them.

4   The top of the dresser has a curved front rail to add both rigidity and an authentic traditional design. At the ends you need to cut stub tenons to fit into the housing joints at the tops of the end panels. First cut the piece of timber to length and then mark out the shoulder lines for the tenons as explained on page

101. Next set your mortice gauge to the width of the housing slot and use it to scribe the width of the tenon. Double check all your markings by 'offering up' the rail to the end panels. Scribble over the 'cheeks' of the tenon that need to be cut away. Then cut out the tenons as described on page 101.

5   Assemble all the joints 'dry' to check your progress. When you are happy with the fit you can cut the shaping on the top front rail and on the 2 end panels. For this I would advise using a coping saw, jigsaw or band saw to cut out the basic shape and then a spokeshave to remove all the saw cuts and finish off the curves. A piece of dowel rod wrapped in glasspaper is also useful here.

To lighten the appearance of the dresser I cut chamfers on both front edges of the end panels and on the underside of the shelves using a chisel. (You could also use a spokeshave, a jack plane or an electric router fitted with the appropriate cutter.) Once all the shaping has been done, use a very sharp smoothing plane to remove any marks or pencil lines from these pieces of wood and the 2 shelves.

6   Assemble the framework 'dry' (without glue) using sash cramps to hold everything in place. Check that it is square by placing a long batten of wood diagonally from corner to corner. Mark off the corners in pencil on the batten and then place it across the other diagonal. If your pencil marks line up with these 2 corners, the framework is square. If it isn't, tap all the joints firmly using a piece of waste wood and a hammer. If it still isn't square you need to re-check all your measurements and make adjustments as necessary.

When you are happy with the framework, apply glue to all the joints and cramp up. Check for squareness again and, if all is well, tighten the cramps. Leave until the glue has cured (dried), then remove any residue of glue with a chisel and smoothing plane. Finally, glue an edging strip along the front of the upper shelf.

7   For the top of the dresser you need to cut a piece of timber to size and then plane a chamfer on the front and side edges. Glue this to the top of the framework.

8 To provide support for the top of the back panelling, glue a batten of wood in place under the top and between the 2 end panels.

9 To finish off the top properly I added a decorative cornice. For this you need to cut mitres and if you have not done this before study the advice on page 102 as it can be a tricky job.

Plane a length of timber so that it is smooth and clean and cut a bevel on the underside using a jack plane (see page 98).

Mark out the 45° mitre joints as explained on page 102 and cut your 3 pieces of cornice from this batten using a tenon saw and mitre block. Double-check your marking out before you cut!

Glue the cornice in position on top of the dresser using G cramps to hold it whilst the glue cures.

10 For the back panelling you simply need to select attractive tongue-and-groove panelling and cut it to length. The boards then fit into the rebate you cut on the end panels and are supported at the top by the cross batten. They should be screwed into position but it is only necessary to screw every 3rd panel in place as the tongue-and-groove shaping holds the boards together. The screws

pass into the cross batten at the top and the back edge of the bottom shelf.

Book Shelf

This optional feature would be very useful if you intend to hang the dresser over a work surface in the kitchen. It will support an open cookery book at a convenient height for the user.

1 Cut out the shelf itself and the batten that has to be attached to it at the back with a length of piano hinge. Piano hinge is available from ironmongers or DIY specialists. It usually comes in 4 foot (1.2m) lengths, but don't worry – there are other projects in this book where you can use the excess (see pages 19 and 69).

Screw the hinge to the 2 pieces of timber.

2 Now cut out the batten for the front edge of the shelf which will prevent the book from sliding off. Shape the ends using a coping saw to remove the corners and a spokeshave to round them off. Glue the batten to the shelf and set it aside for the glue to cure.

Cut out the 2 blocks that will support the shelf in the closed position and glue these to the underside.

3 The shelf is held in position under the dresser by 2 fairly substantial support brackets. Cut 2 pieces of timber to length and then mark and cut out the

recess on each which will accommodate the batten on the back of the shelf. You will need to offer up this batten to the finished recess to check that the depth will allow it to move back and forwards smoothly. Use glasspaper and then candle grease on the recesses and the ends of the shelf batten to get a good sliding action.

4 Before fixing the brackets and shelf to the dresser, cut out and shape a handle for the shelf and glue it in position. Use a sharp chisel to achieve the gentle depressions on either side of this handle that will help fingers to grip it.

5 With the back batten of the shelf 'trapped' in the recesses of the support brackets, screw the brackets to the underside of the bottom shelf of the dresser.

6 Finally, cut a further length of batten and screw this to the underside of the front of the brackets. This provides the support for the shelf when it is pulled out and in use.

Several coats of clear polyurethane varnish with a careful glasspapering in between would be a very good idea for this piece of furniture if it is to be used in the kitchen. If, however, you intend to use it somewhere where grease and/or water are unlikely to come into contact with it, I recommend good-quality furniture polish and loving care!

Cutting list

End panel	2 off	765 × 229 × 22mm (30⅛ × 9 × ⅞in)	Timber
Top front cross rail	1 off	816 × 152 × 25mm (32⅛ × 6 × 1in)	Timber
Upper shelf	1 off	816 × 137 × 22mm (32⅛ × 5⅜ × ⅞in)	Timber
Lower shelf	1 off	816 × 213 × 22mm (32⅛ × 8⅜ × ⅞in)	Timber
Edging strip	1 off	794 × 32 × 9mm (31¼ × 1¼ × ⅜in)	Timber
Top	1 off	908 × 194 × 16mm (35¾ × 7⅝ × ⅝in)	Timber
	1 off	794 × 25 × 25mm (31¼ × 1 × 1in)	Timber
Cornice	1 off	946 × 54 × 22mm (37¼ × 2⅛ × ⅞in)	Timber
	2 off	213 × 54 × 22mm (8⅜ × 2⅛ × ⅞in)	Timber
Back panelling	10 off	689 × 92 × 16mm (27⅛ × 3⅝ × ⅝in)	Tongue-and-groove board
Shelf support runner	1 off	448 × 51 × 22mm (17⅝ × 2 × ⅞in)	Timber
	2 off	213 × 57 × 25mm (8⅜ × 2¼ × 1in)	Timber
Book shelf	1 off	394 × 191 × 20mm (15½ × 7½ × ¾in)	Timber
	1 off	448 × 35 × 18mm (17⅝ × 1⅜ × ¹¹⁄₁₆in)	Timber
	1 off	470 × 32 × 22mm (18½ × 1¼ × ⅞in)	Timber
	1 off	178 × 28 × 22mm (7 × 1⅛ × ⅞in)	Timber
	2 off	105 × 38 × 25mm (4⅛ × 1½ × 1in)	Timber
Ancillaries			
	1 off	381mm (15in) long × 20mm (¾in) piano hinge	

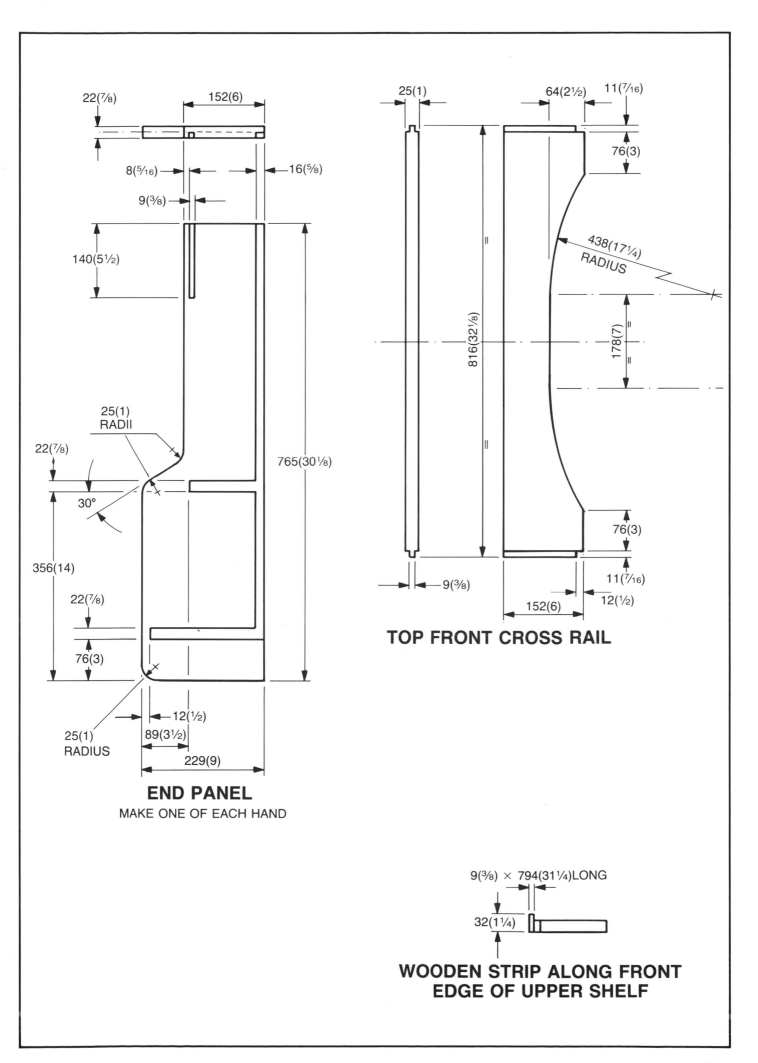

END PANEL
MAKE ONE OF EACH HAND

TOP FRONT CROSS RAIL

WOODEN STRIP ALONG FRONT EDGE OF UPPER SHELF

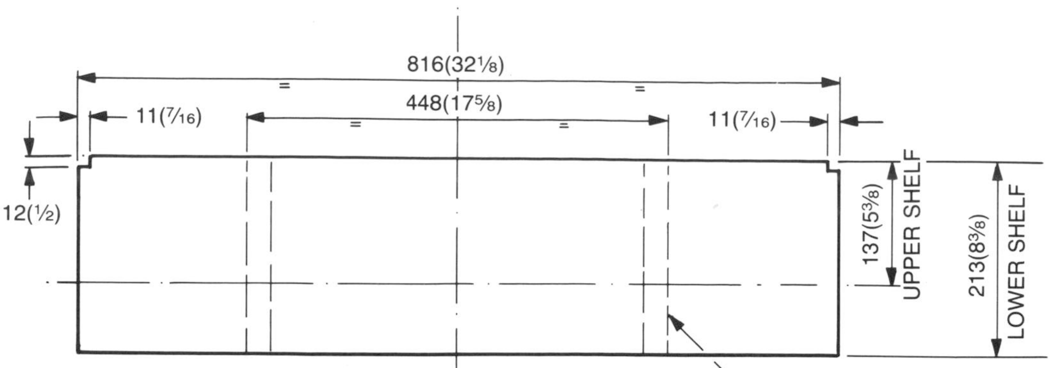
816(32⅛)
448(17⅝)
11(7/16)
11(7/16)
12(½)
137(5⅜)
UPPER SHELF
213(8⅜)
LOWER SHELF
POSITION OF SLIDING BOOK SUPPORT RUNNER ASSEMBLY ON UNDERSIDE OF LOWER SHELF

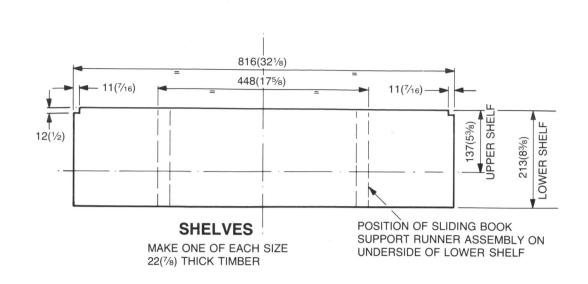

SHELVES

MAKE ONE OF EACH SIZE
22(⅞) THICK TIMBER

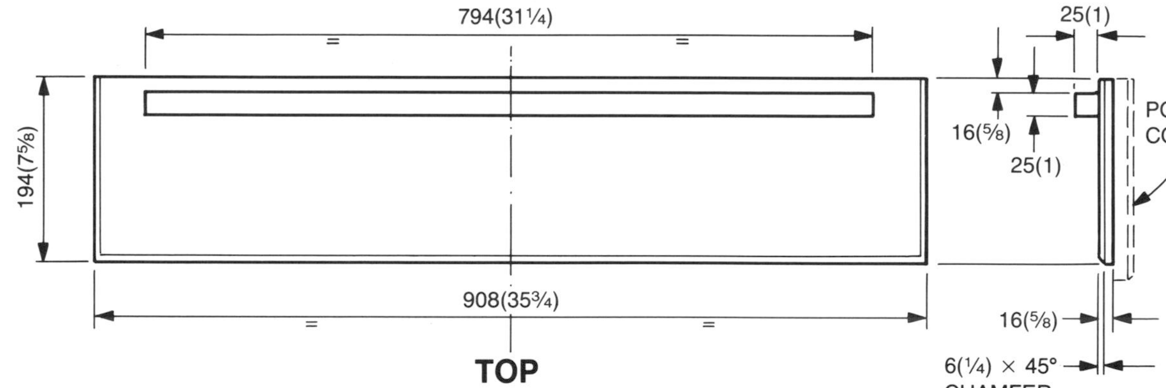
794(31¼)
194(7⅝)
908(35¾)
25(1)
16(⅝)
25(1)
POSITION OF CORNICE
16(⅝)
6(¼) × 45° CHAMFER

TOP

(VIEW ON UNDERSIDE)

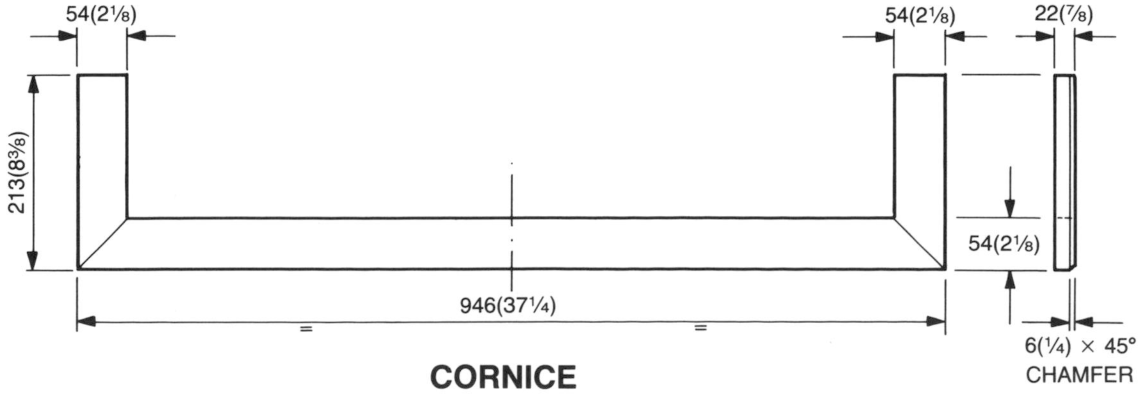
54(2⅛)
54(2⅛)
22(⅞)
213(8⅜)
54(2⅛)
946(37¼)
6(¼) × 45° CHAMFER

CORNICE

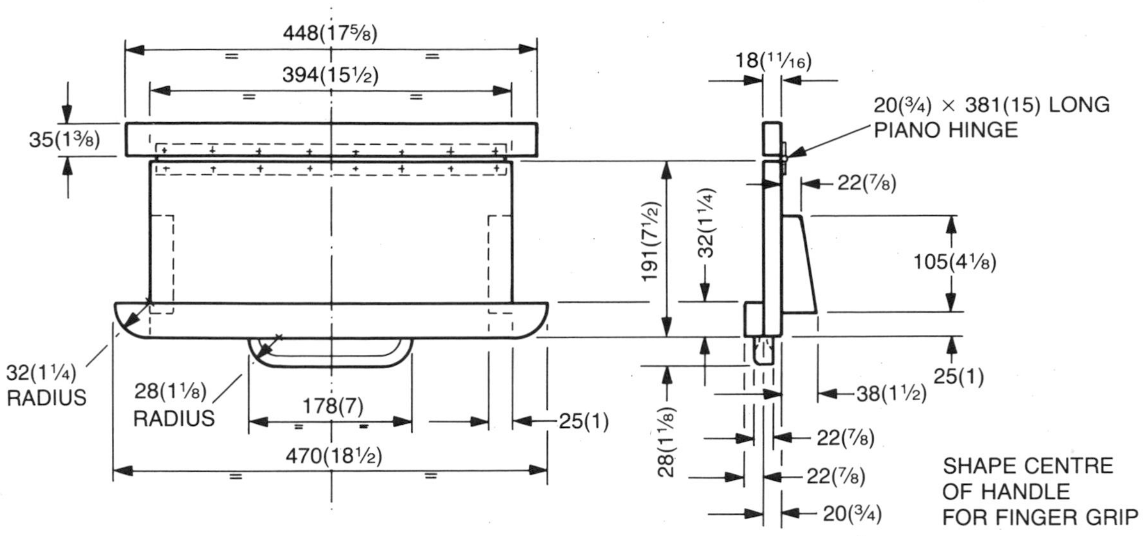
448(17⅝)
394(15½)
35(1⅜)
32(1¼)
RADIUS
28(1⅛)
RADIUS
178(7)
25(1)
470(18½)
191(7½)
32(1¼)
28(1⅛)
18(11/16)
20(¾) × 381(15) LONG
PIANO HINGE
22(⅞)
105(4⅛)
25(1)
38(1½)
22(⅞)
22(⅞)
20(¾)
SHAPE CENTRE
OF HANDLE
FOR FINGER GRIP

SLIDING BOOK SUPPORT ASSEMBLY

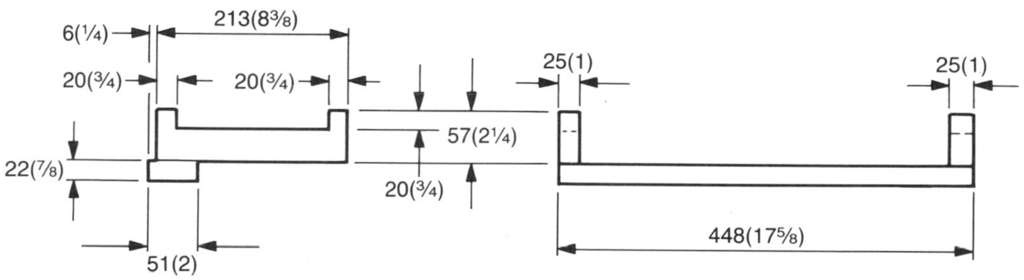
6(¼)
213(8⅜)
20(¾)
20(¾)
22(⅞)
57(2¼)
20(¾)
51(2)
25(1)
25(1)
448(17⅝)

SLIDING BOOK SUPPORT RUNNER ASSEMBLY

SHELVING UNIT

Many of us have items that we treasure and love to look at. Everyone has favourite books that they enjoy browsing through too, and this free-standing shelving unit is ideal for both. It is designed so that you can choose the type of shelves you prefer from either the wide range of colours available in melamine-faced chipboard, or solid timber. Nordic pine shelving is readily available at good timber stores and builders' merchants, but try to avoid parana pine; it is extremely expensive and tends to be more difficult to get a good finish on.

I chose to make the main framework from whitewood which contrasts well with the black ash-faced chipboard shelves. However, be warned that whitewood is not as easy to work as pine and you have to be especially careful to avoid knots in load-bearing sections of the main frames.

The main joint used is a twin mortice and tenon (see page 101). The twin tenon is needed for extra strength as the pieces of wood used are quite narrow. The twin tenons are stopped – in other words, they don't go right through the uprights. The cross rail pieces in the uprights serve a dual purpose. They hold the uprights together and support the shelves.

1 Study the working drawings carefully before you buy your wood and take time at the timber merchant's to choose your wood carefully, especially the pieces for the uprights.

2 Having picked your wood for the basic framework start by making the 4 frames, 2 tall ones and 2 shorter ones. Mark and cut out the 4 long verticals together, then the 4 shorter verticals. For the cross rails you need 8 of the same length for the shorter frames and 12 of the same length for the tall frames. Mark the face side and face edge on each piece (see page 99).

3 Once the pieces for the frames have been cut to length you can start on the twin mortice and tenon joints. Use sash cramps or masking tape to hold the uprights together for 1 set of frames and mark out the position of all the mortice holes using a carpenter's square and pencil (see page 101). Repeat the procedure with the verticals for the other set of frames.

Now, cramp or tape the cross rails together for 1 pair of frames and pencil in all the shoulder lines for the twin tenons. It is vital to mark these out together and as accurately as you can, otherwise the frames simply won't fit together. Repeat the procedure for the second set of frames. Separate the pieces and continue the shoulder lines right round each cross rail.

As a final check, assemble the pieces for each frame on the floor so that you are sure you will not later discover the problem of a couple of large mortice holes in the wrong place.

4 Satisfied that you have pencilled the mortice and tenons in correctly, you can now cut in all the shoulder lines on the rails using a marking knife (see page 101). Then set up your mortice gauge and mark in the width of the mortice holes and tenons as described on page 101. Remember that once you have set the gauge to the correct chisel width you can use it to mark both mortice and tenon. Also remember that you need 2 of each as these are *twin* mortice and tenon joints.

5 Now cut out all the mortice and tenons following the instructions and advice on page 101. Remember that the mortice holes are stopped – don't cut right through the wood. A very sharp chisel and good solid work bench are essential for this tricky job.

6 Before you can assemble the frames you have one more joint to cut on the cross rails. Each of the inner rails (4 on the tall frames, 2 on the shorter ones) has to have a halving joint to take the shelf supports.

First cut out the 2 long and 2 short shelf supports and then mark and cut out the halving joints on these and the cross rails at the same time, following the instructions on page 100. When these are glued and screwed across the 4 vertical frames they will add rigidity to the whole unit as well as providing extra support for the shelves.

7 Once all the joints have been cut you are ready to assemble the 4 vertical frames. First use a sharp smoothing plane (see page 105) to work over all the rails and uprights and remove any pencil lines or finger marks.

After this 'cleaning up' operation, assemble the frames 'dry' (without glue) and check for squareness by laying a long batten or dowel rod diagonally from corner to corner. Mark each corner off on the batten and then lay it across the other 2 corners. If the pencil marks do not line up with the corners your frame is not square, and you need to check all your measurements again!

Once you are sure each frame is square, take them to pieces and, one by one, apply glue and cramp up using sash cramps (see page 103). Again check for squareness and, if necessary, slacken the cramps and angle the heads to pull the frame into square. Once you have got this right, tighten the cramps and leave the glue to cure (dry) according to the manufacturer's instructions.

8 Now you are ready to make the base or 'plinth'. Cut the 4 pieces of timber to length and mark out the twin mortice and tenons as described above. You also need to mark out rebates (half a halving joint, if you like) on the underside of each of the long pieces which will later accommodate the 2 central frames.

Knife in and then cut out all these joints, assemble dry and check for squareness as explained above. Then apply glue to the mortice and tenon joints, cramp the plinth together, check for squareness again and leave until the glue has cured.

9 Once the vertical frames have dried, you can embark on adding the decorative grooves that run round their face sides. Whether you use a chisel and a hand router or an electric router (see page 98) for this job, it is a very good idea to cramp a piece of extra timber along the full length of the frame to give the tool extra width to work on. Otherwise the narrowness of the frame might lead to the router slipping off and damaging your handiwork or, worse, you. It does take a while to set this up before each pass is made with the machine, but it is time well spent. Also, be careful not to cut the grooves too deep or you may expose the mortice and tenon joints.

The entire routing operation takes time but does add a very attractive finish.

10 At last you are ready to screw the frames to the plinth. Although it is more fiddly, if you screw from the inside of the plinth into the frames the screws will all be hidden. Alternatively, you could screw from the face side and face edges of the frames into the plinth and disguise the heads by counterboring the holes and plugging them (see page 104).

11 Now glue and screw the shelf supports in place via the halving joints that you cut previously.

12 Finally you are ready to cut the shelves to the required length and width. If you are using melamine-faced board rather than solid timber I advise you to use a jigsaw fitted with a metal-cutting blade or an electric saw fitted with a tungsten carbide blade (see page 98) as it is not easy to cut this without chipping the facing.

If you decide to add a lip to the back of the shelves as I have you need to cut out these narrow pieces of board too.

13 Once you have cut all your board to size you need to cover the cut edges with strips of matching veneer.

Cut a strip slightly longer than the edge you wish to cover. Heat a (preferably old!) electric iron and then, holding the strip in place on the edge with your fingers, iron along the strip so that the glue melts and bonds it to the board. (It's really quite simple – much easier than ironing a shirt!)

Once the glue has cooled and cured you may need to remove any excess strip. This can be done in a number of ways:
i using a very sharp chisel at an angle and working along the length of the shelf;
ii using a marking knife with a *new blade*. Hold the knife so that you are cutting as near to the handle as possible;

iii using the appropriate cutter in an electric router. This works beautifully but is an expensive extra unless you intend to use it a lot.

14 Now screw the lip (if using) onto the back of the shelves from the underside. All the screwholes need to be counter bored (see page 104) so that the screw heads lie just beneath the surface of the board.

15 Before fitting the shelves, finish the framework with two coats of clear polyurethane varnish, glasspapering the wood carefully after each coat. I found a lint-free rag was the best means of getting the varnish into the grooves without ending up with unsightly globules running down the frame.

16 Once the varnish has dried completely you can simply lay the finished shelves in place. However, if you screw them in position you will add rigidity to the frame and also avoid them being dislodged accidentally.

I used a new type of screw called a Multi (see page 104) to screw the shelves down. This has a square slot in the head and needs a special screwdriver to fix it, but its shape, and the fact that it comes in a range of colours to match your board, means that it is not so noticeable as an ordinary screw.

Cutting list

Plinth	2 off	1441 × 44 × 22mm (56¾ × 1¾ × ⅞in)		Timber
	2 off	267 × 44 × 22mm (10½ × 1¾ × ⅞in)		Timber
Tall frame	4 off	1892 × 44 × 22mm (74½ × 1¾ × ⅞in)		Timber
	12 off	312 × 44 × 22mm (12¼ × 1¾ × ⅞in)		Timber
Short frame	4 off	1753 × 44 × 22mm (69 × 1¾ × ⅞in)		Timber
	8 off	185 × 44 × 22mm (7¼ × 1¾ × ⅞in)		Timber
Shelf support	2 off	1486 × 44 × 22mm (58½ × 1¾ × ⅞in)		Timber
	2 off	578 × 44 × 22mm (22¾ × 1¾ × ⅞in)		Timber
Long shelf	3 off	1441 × 279 × 14mm (56¾ × 11 × ⁹⁄₁₆in)		Chipboard
	2 off	1441 × 25 × 14mm (56¾ × 1 × ⁹⁄₁₆in)		Chipboard
Short shelf	2 off	622 × 279 × 14mm (24½ × 11 × ⁹⁄₁₆in)		Chipboard
	2 off	622 × 25 × 14mm (24½ × 1 × ⁹⁄₁₆in)		Chipboard

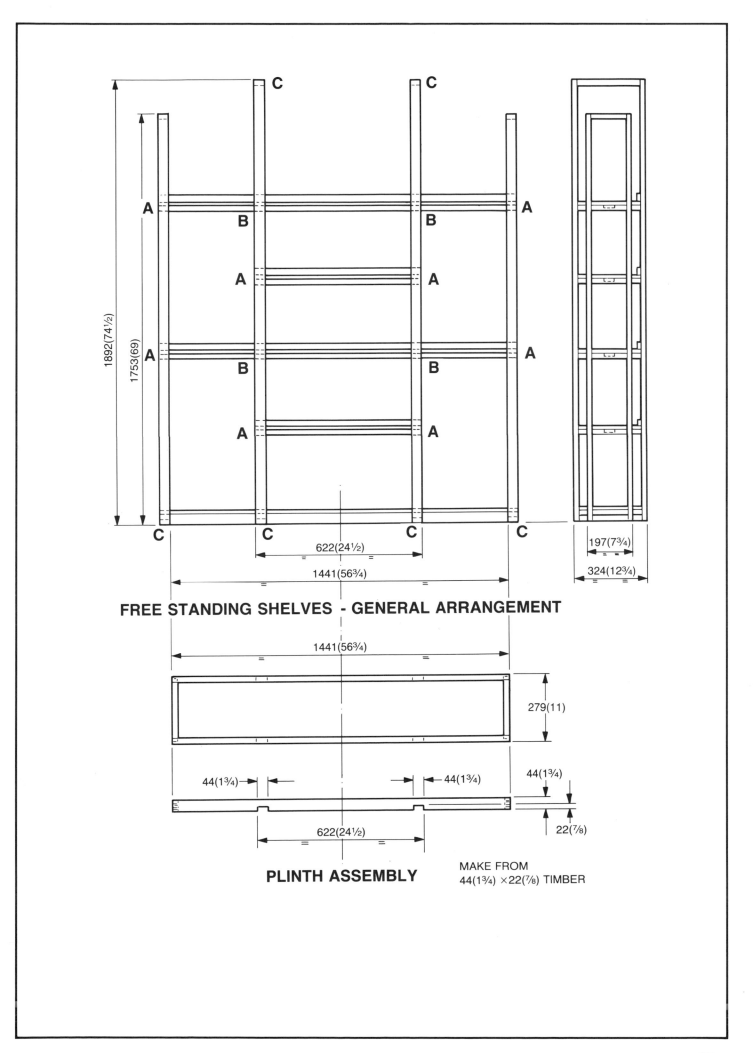

1892(74½)

1753(69)

A

B

A

A

B

A

C

C

C

C

C

C

622(24½)

1441(56¾)

197(7¾)

324(12¾)

FREE STANDING SHELVES - GENERAL ARRANGEMENT

1441(56¾)

279(11)

44(1¾)

44(1¾)

44(1¾)

622(24½)

22(⅞)

PLINTH ASSEMBLY

MAKE FROM
44(1¾) ×22(⅞) TIMBER

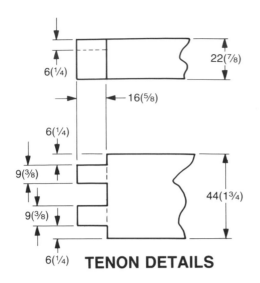

TENON DETAILS

6(¼)

22(⅞)

16(⅝)

6(¼)

9(⅜)

44(1¾)

9(⅜)

6(¼)

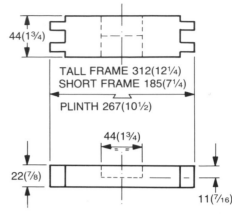

44(1¾)

TALL FRAME 312(12¼)
SHORT FRAME 185(7¼)

PLINTH 267(10½)

44(1¾)

22(⅞)

11(⁷⁄₁₆)

PLINTH, UPPER AND LOWER CROSS MEMBERS
HAVE HAUNCHED TWIN TENONS TO BROKEN LINE
OF TENON DETAIL DRAWING WHILE THE
REMAINDER HAVE FULL TWIN TENONS AND HALVING
JOINTS TO THE DOTTED LINES ABOVE

CROSS RAILS

MAKE 12 AT THE 311(12¼) LENGTH
MAKE 8 AT THE 185(7¼) LENGTH
MAKE 2 AT THE 267(10½) LENGTH

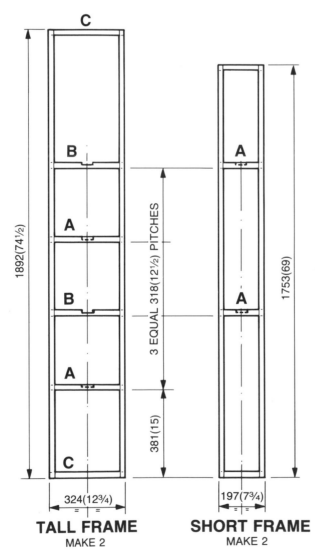

C

B

A

B

A

C

1892(74½)

3 EQUAL 318(12½) PITCHES

381(15)

324(12¾)

TALL FRAME
MAKE 2

A

A

1753(69)

197(7¾)

SHORT FRAME
MAKE 2

MAKE BOTH PAIR OF FRAMES IN 44(1¾) × 22(⅞) TIMBER
MORTICE VERTICALS TO SUIT CROSS RAIL

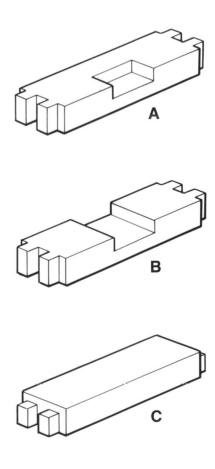

A

B

C

PICTORIAL VIEWS
OF CROSS RAILS
(not to scale)

Teak-faced blanket chest

Welsh dresser

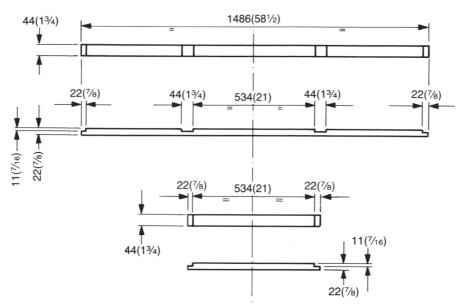

SHELF SUPPORTS
MAKE 2 OF EACH LENGTH

MAKE FROM 14(9/16) THICK BLACK ASH FACED CHIPBOARD

SHORT SHELF 622(24½) MAKE 2

LONG SHELF AND
PLINTH TOP 1441(56¾) MAKE 3

SHELVES AND PLINTH TOP
NOTE THERE IS NO REAR
LIP ON PLINTH TOP

The traditional cabinet joint that professionals would use for this type of cupboard is very specialised. I have tried to make the unit look traditional and yet to find ways round the complex joints used by the super-craftsmen.

The dimensions are not critical, so if you are re-fitting your kitchen, you can adapt the various lengths and widths to suit the size of the room. It is also possible to adapt the door frames and have a set of, say, 4 or even 6 doors. The worktop could be either a pine-faced plywood fitted with a pine bullnose moulding or you could fit a length of standard worktop from one of the large DIY stores.

The unit involves 2 main joints – halving joints, and mortice and tenon joints for the doors. But what really makes it look traditional is the pine tongue-and-groove panelling set into rebates at the back of each frame.

Before starting work, check the various mains in your kitchen – water, gas pipes, wirings, etc – and see if you need to make allowances for them. The unit consists of 6 sections: 1 front (including 2 doors), 2 sides, 1 back, 1 base, 1 top and 1 plinth.

1 The plinth is made from 6 pieces of wood. Adjust its width if necessary to allow pipes to run along the back.

After cutting the pieces to length, mark the full thickness of the side pieces onto the ends of the front and back pieces for rebate joints. After working over the pencil lines with a marking knife, cut the rebates. This can be done in a variety of ways:
i by cutting down the shoulder line with a tenon saw and chiselling away the waste with a firmer chisel;
ii by using a rebate plane;
iii by using an electric router (see page 98).
When the rebates have been cut, apply glue to the joints and assemble the plinth. Check for squareness (see page 23, step 6) and cramp up using sash cramps.

When the glue has cured, glue the remaining 2 battens onto the inside of the plinth sides.

2 Now make the back panel. This is a framework of timber which is then fitted with a backing of plywood. The framework is made using halving joints which are very versatile and well worth mastering.

Cut out the 4 pieces of timber and mark out the halving joints following the instructions on page 100. (I always use the timber itself to mark out the width needed as this is more accurate than measuring with a rule.) Make sure you go over all the pencil lines carefully with a marking knife before you start to cut, otherwise you won't achieve a neat shoulder line.

Cut out the halving joints following the method described on page 100.

3 While you are 'in the mood' make the frameworks for the 2 end panels now too. These are made in exactly the same way – 4 pieces of timber held together with halving joints – except that you also need to cut a rebate on the back inside edge of each piece of timber. These will provide the recesses into which you will later fit the tongue-and-groove panelling, so it is a good idea to buy this before you cut the rebate to make sure it is the right depth.

Note that the rebates on the 2 uprights are 'through', i.e. they are cut right along from end to end of the timber, but on the top and bottom piece of timber for each framework they are 'stopped', i.e. they finish in right-angled corners. This is so that the rebates won't show on the sides of the end panels. Double check all your marking out to ensure you have marked the correct rebates in position and on the right side of the wood. Cut the through rebates first and 'offer up' the uprights to the top and bottom pieces so that you can be certain you have measured the stopped rebates correctly.

As I explained above (step 1), you can cut rebates in a variety of ways. However, note that if you use hand tools (i.e. tenon saw and chisel, or rebate plane) you need to cut the rebates *before* you glue up the frame. If you use an electric router you can glue up the framework and, once the glue has cured, cut the entire rebate in one operation. Also note that a rebate plane won't cut the 'stopped' rebates completely as the depth gauge prevents the tool from cutting the right angle. You will therefore need to chop out the ends with a chisel and use a bullnose plane to finish the joint.

When all the halving joints and rebates have been cut, assemble the back and end frames 'dry' to check for fit and squareness.

4 Before you actually glue up the end panel frames I would recommend cutting a chamfer on all the inside edges of the timber. It is a small detail but it makes a great difference to the overall appearance of the cupboard. Remove the corner edge from each piece of timber using a chisel and then use a spokeshave (see page 105) to finish rounding off the wood neatly. Alternatively an electric router will do the job quickly but if you use this tool it is a good idea to buy a router with a small bearing at the bottom of the cutting bit. This rests on the wood and allows the cutter to run freely. Ordinary cutters do have a steel guide pin but you have to move the router quickly otherwise this pin burns the wood. If you haven't cut chamfers before, experiment on waste wood until you are happy with your technique.

5 Now glue and cramp up the back frame and end frames, check for squareness and, if all is well, tighten the sash cramps and leave for the glue to cure.

6 Finish off the back panel by fitting a piece of plywood to the framework. This can be glued, screwed or panel-pinned in place.

7 Cut to length and fit tongue-and-groove pine boards into the rebates on the frames for the end panels. I panel-pinned these in position from the inside as pins will allow the wood to expand and contract without splitting. (Note: It is a good idea to treat these boards with polyurethane varnish before you fit them. Otherwise if the wood 'moves' at a later stage you might end up with a line of un-varnished wood showing.)

8 Now for the base. This is a piece of pine-faced plywood (available from DIY stores and timber merchants) that has to be cut to length. To cover up the exposed plywood edges, glue and panel-pin pine bullnosed moulding in place round the front and sides. Ideally these should be mitred where they meet at the corners (see page 102).

9 You can now assemble the carcass of the unit as follows:
i Screw the plinth to the base by passing screws through the battens glued inside the sides of the plinth up into the base board.
ii Drill pilot holes down the sides of the back panel framework. Pass screws from the back of the back panel, via the pilot holes, into the back edges of the end panel frames.
iii Attach the base to the end and back panels by passing screws from underneath the base into the bottom edges of the frames.

10 Once the carcass is complete you can turn your attention to the front frame and doors. The frame comprises 3 upright pieces of timber and 1 cross piece for the top.

Cut the 4 pieces of timber to length and cut the rebates on the ends of the cross piece which will accommodate the outer uprights. You also need to mark carefully and cut out a recess in the centre into which the central upright has to be fixed. Use the uprights themselves to mark the width and depth of these joints accurately. When you have cut out all the joints glue the framework together.

Fit the framework in place by driving screws through the outer uprights into

the side panels. Note from the plans that it should be set back far enough for the front of the doors (when they are fitted) to be flush with the front of the side panels. For extra rigidity fix the centre upright to the floor by means of a small block of wood which you can glue and/or screw in place.

11 Each door consists of a frame filled in with tongue-and-groove panelling similar in appearance to the end panels. However, the joints used for the frames are mortice and tenons which are complicated slightly by the need to cut a rebate again right round the inner edge of the frame to accommodate the infill panelling.

As you want to conceal the ends of the rebate grooves so that they can't be seen when the doors are opened, the shoulders of the tenon have to be different in length. Study the drawing on page 43 and the instructions for cutting mortice and tenon joints on page 101 and practise on waste wood until you are confident. Pencilling on the face side and face edge marks (see page 99) and careful marking out are essential. I would advise cutting the mortice hole first, then cutting down the cheeks of the tenon but not removing the waste at this stage. Next cut the rebate as described on page 39 and, finally, remove the tenon cheeks. It is particularly important to check that you are cutting the rebate on the correct edge.

When the joints have been cut, glue the frame together checking for squareness as usual before you tighten up the sash cramps.

12 Fit the tongue-and-groove boards into the rebate on the back of each door and panel pin them in place from the inside. To conceal the pin heads, use a panel pin punch and a light hammer to drive them just below the surface of the wood and fill the holes with Brummer stopping (available from DIY stores). This comes in a variety of colours so make sure you choose the right one.

13 The doors are attached to the front frame using traditional brass hinges which have to be recessed. To do this, pencil round a hinge flap in the necessary 3 positions on the inside of the door frame and then set your marking gauge to the thickness of the flap. Use the gauge to scribe this thickness on the sides of the frame to give you the depth of the recesses required.

Next set the gauge to the width of the flap plus *half* the hinge pin and

transfer this width onto the outer uprights of the front frame. Use a marking knife to etch in all the pencil and gauge lines firmly and then remove the waste wood using a bevel-edged chisel. This is a delicate job requiring patience and a light touch. Ease the wood out carefully and keep offering up the hinges to the recesses to check the fit.

When the hinge recesses are finished, screw the doors in place. It is important to drill pilot holes when using brass screws as they are soft and may break off. Screw the hinges to the doors first and then fit the doors on the cupboard.

14 To finish off the doors you will need to screw on knobs or handles – I used brass but white ceramic or matching pine would also look attractive. In addition, you need to screw on magnetic catches to keep the doors closed.

15 As I said in the introduction to this project, the type of top you fit is, of course, your choice. If you decide to use pine-faced plywood, first cut the top to size using a jigsaw fitted with a metal-cutting blade or an electric saw fitted with a tungsten carbide blade (see page 98) to avoid chipping the pine facing. Then cut pine bullnosed moulding to length to glue and pin round the edge of the top to conceal the exposed plywood. As with the base this edging really ought to be mitred at the corners (see page 102).

Glue battens of wood right round inside the top of the cupboard and then screw the top to these battens by passing screws up from underneath them into the plywood. Make sure you use the right length of screw so that the ends do not show under the pine facing, or worse, break through.

Should you decide to make a top in solid pine it is best to use boards no wider than 102mm (4in), otherwise the timber is likely to 'move'. Boards 51mm (2in) wide would be ideal. Join the boards using dowels and glue as explained on page 103.

Screw the finished top on via battens of wood as described above.

Whatever type of top you make allow an overhang of about 20mm (¾in) at the sides and front.

16 I used 2 coats of an acrylic varnish to seal and protect the wood. This is very easy to apply and dries quickly. Glasspaper the first coat carefully and remove the dust before you apply the second.

Cutting list

Plinth	2 off	1035 × 114 × 25mm (40¾ × 4½ × 1in)	Timber
	2 off	508 × 114 × 25mm (20 × 4½ × 1in)	Timber
	2 off	483 × 35 × 28mm (19 × 1⅜ × 1⅛in)	Timber
Back panel	2 off	1054 × 70 × 32mm (41½ × 2¾ × 1¼in)	Timber
	2 off	816 × 38 × 32mm (32⅛ × 1½ × 1¼in)	Timber
	1 off	1054 × 816 × 12mm (41½ × 32⅛ × ½in)	Plywood
End panels	4 off	816 × 70 × 32mm (32⅛ × 2¾ × 1¼in)	Timber
	4 off	565 × 70 × 32mm (22¼ × 2¾ × 1¼in)	Timber
	10 off	700 × 92 × 12mm (27⅝ × 3⅝ × ½in)	Tongue-and-groove board
Front frame	2 off	816 × 51 × 38mm (32⅛ × 2 × 1½in)	Timber
	1 off	1054 × 70 × 32mm (41½ × 2¾ × 1¼in)	Timber
	1 off	816 × 70 × 32mm (32⅛ × 2¾ × 1¼in)	Timber
	1 off	76 × 70 × 32mm (3 × 2¾ × 1¼in)	Timber
Base	1 off	1092 × 552 × 12mm (43 × 21¾ × ½in)	Plywood
	1 off	1118 × 12 × 12mm (44 × ½ × ½in)	Bull-nosed moulding
	2 off	565 × 12 × 12mm (22¼ × ½ × ½in)	Bull-nosed moulding
Door	4 off	711 × 70 × 32mm (28 × 2¾ × 1¼in)	Timber
	4 off	483 × 70 × 32mm (19 × 2¾ × 1¼in)	Timber
	8 off	659 × 92 × 12mm (26 × 3⅝ × ½in)	Tongue-and-groove board
Top surface	1 off	1118 × 565 × 12mm (44 × 22¼ × ½in)	Plywood
	2 off	585 × 25 × 20mm (23 × 1 × ¾in)	Bull-nosed moulding
	1 off	1158 × 25 × 20mm (45½ × 1 × ¾in)	Bull-nosed moulding

Ancillaries

	6 off	51mm (2in) brass hinges
	2 off	Decorative handles and fasteners

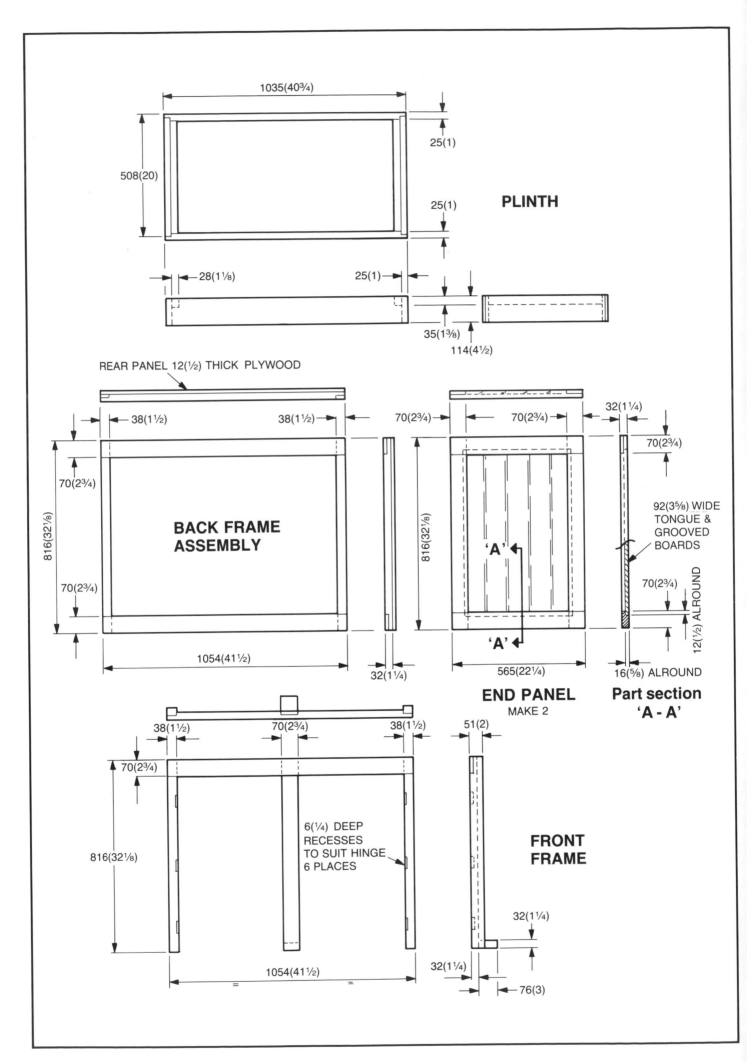

1035(40¾)

25(1)

508(20)

PLINTH

25(1)

28(1⅛)   25(1)

35(1⅜)

114(4½)

REAR PANEL 12(½) THICK PLYWOOD

38(1½)   38(1½)

70(2¾)   70(2¾)

32(1¼)

70(2¾)

816(32⅛)

816(32⅛)

**BACK FRAME
ASSEMBLY**

92(3⅝) WIDE
TONGUE &
GROOVED
BOARDS

'A'

70(2¾)

70(2¾)

70(2¾)

12(½) ALROUND

1054(41½)

32(1¼)

'A'

565(22¼)

16(⅝) ALROUND

END PANEL
MAKE 2

**Part section
'A - A'**

38(1½)   70(2¾)   38(1½)

51(2)

70(2¾)

**FRONT
FRAME**

816(32⅛)

6(¼) DEEP
RECESSES
TO SUIT HINGE
6 PLACES

32(1¼)

1054(41½)

32(1¼)

76(3)

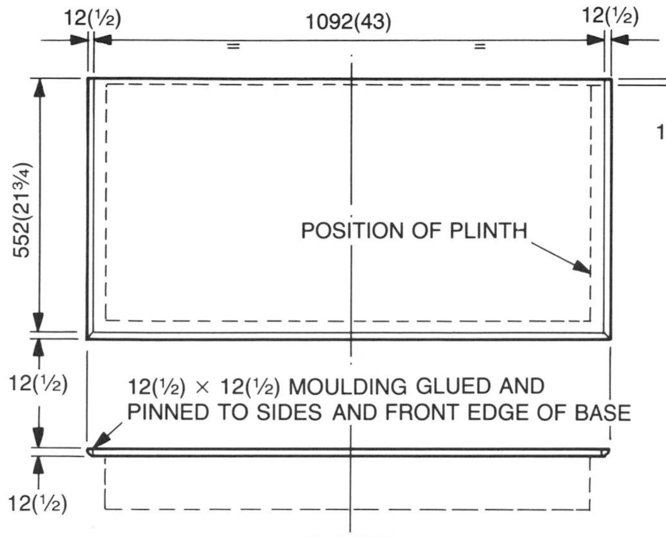
12(½)
1092(43)
12(½)
12(½)
552(21¾)
POSITION OF PLINTH
12(½)
12(½) × 12(½) MOULDING GLUED AND PINNED TO SIDES AND FRONT EDGE OF BASE
12(½)

BASE

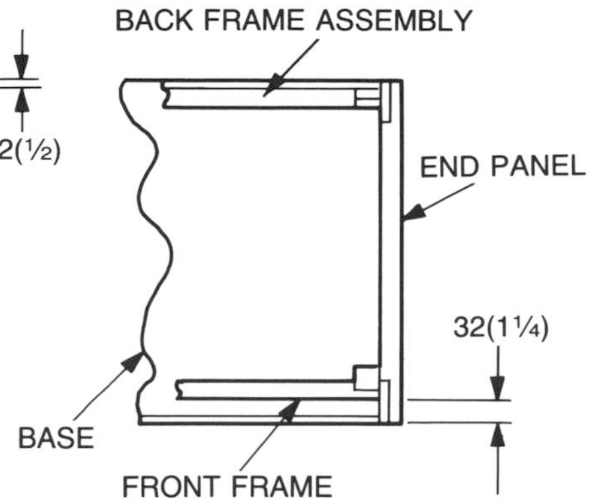
BACK FRAME ASSEMBLY
END PANEL
32(1¼)
BASE
FRONT FRAME

Part plan view illustrating carcass build-up

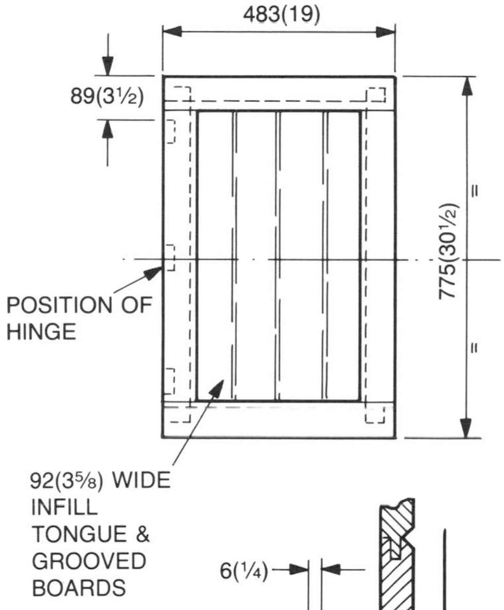
483(19)
89(3½)
775(30½)
POSITION OF HINGE
92(3⅝) WIDE INFILL TONGUE & GROOVED BOARDS

DOOR
MAKE 2

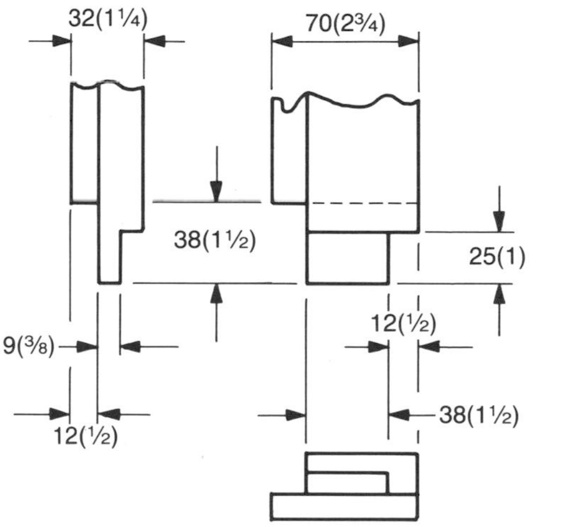
32(1¼)
70(2¾)
38(1½)
25(1)
12(½)
9(⅜)
38(1½)
12(½)

Typical vertical door frame tenon

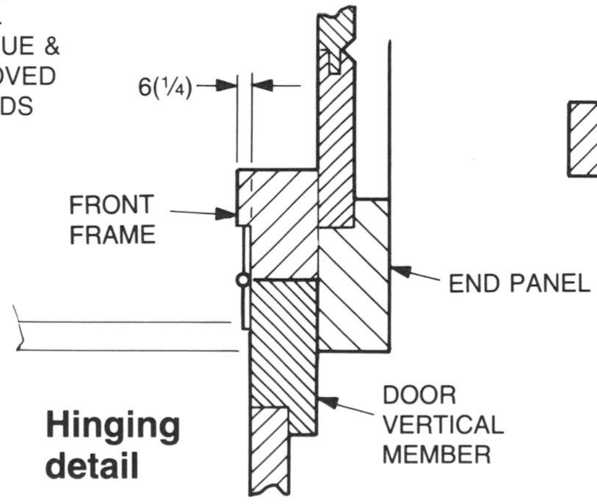
6(¼)
FRONT FRAME
END PANEL
DOOR VERTICAL MEMBER

Hinging detail

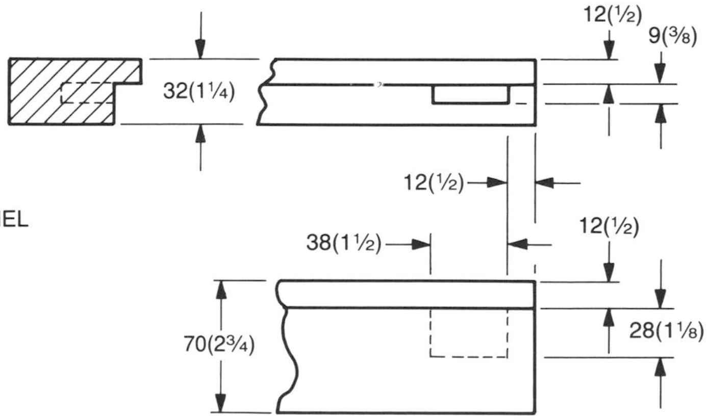
12(½)
9(⅜)
32(1¼)
12(½)
12(½)
38(1½)
70(2¾)
28(1⅛)

Typical mortise in door horizontal members

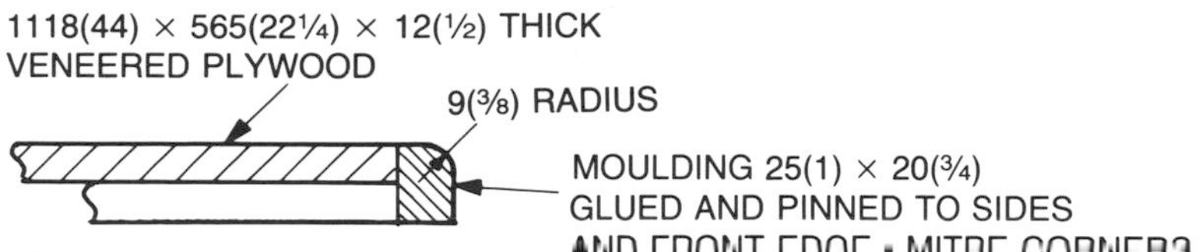
1118(44) × 565(22¼) × 12(½) THICK VENEERED PLYWOOD
9(⅜) RADIUS
MOULDING 25(1) × 20(¾) GLUED AND PINNED TO SIDES AND FRONT EDGE - MITRE CORNERS

TOP SURFACE

This blanket chest is made to a traditional design and much of the construction follows the practices and methods of carpentry laid down by craftsmen over many hundreds of years. Early cabinet-makers quickly discovered that large pieces of wood warped, even when well-seasoned, and it was therefore necessary to devise joinery methods that minimised movement and distortion in furniture. So, frame and panel construction was devised whereby each panel was held securely in a mortice and tenon framework. The panel could still move as it was not glued in place but held in the grooves of the frame. With this method of construction, the panels can both expand and contract without distorting the shape of the furniture.

The only departure from traditional construction methods in this chest is that I used tongue-and-groove panelling for the floor and lid which is readily available from timber merchants. I constructed the chest entirely in Nordic Redwood and am refreshed every time I open the lid by the deep scent of resinous pine. Careful selection of your timber is very important for this project, particularly where the rails are concerned. You don't want any large knots just where you need to plough the grooves to take the panels.

This is not a project for a novice as it does require a substantial amount of woodworking skills. Therefore, if you are inexperienced, it is a good idea to try several of the other, less demanding projects from this book to build up your woodworking skills first.

1 The first sections to tackle are the frames for the front, back and sides of the chest. Study the plans and familiarise yourself with the required joints where the corner posts meet the rails: stopped stub mortice and tenons at the bottom and secret haunched mortice and tenons at the top (see pages 101 and 102). The reason for the joint being hidden at the top is an old woodworking convention that if the top of an upright is going to be exposed (as it is when the lid is lifted) you shouldn't be able to see anything of the joint.

2 Select 4 sturdy pieces of timber for the corner posts and mark face side and face edge on each (see page 99). It is a real necessity to do this on all the wood for this project, not only to ensure that the best sides of the timber face outwards, but also so that you have a visual means of checking you are cutting all the joints in the right places.

Cramp the posts together and mark in pencil the positions for the 2 different types of mortices.

3 Now cut the 4 long rails for the front and back frames, cramp them together and mark in the shoulder lines for the tenons. Separate them and continue the shoulder lines right round each rail.

Then cut out the vertical panel dividers, 2 each for the front and back frames, and pencil in the shoulder lines for the tenons in the same way.

Finally, cut out the 4 end rails for the sides of the chest and, again, cramp them together and pencil in the shoulder lines.

4 Lay all the pieces out on the floor and check carefully that you have marked out all the joints correctly and that the face side and face edges of the timber really will face outwards when the frames are assembled. This planning and checking stage is vital, otherwise you could spend many hours on the project only to find that you have cut a mortice on the wrong side of a corner post or a rail is too short.

5 Once you are sure your marking out is accurate you can knife in the shoulder lines and mark out the mortice holes and tenons with a mortice gauge as explained on page 101.

6 Now comes the lengthy task of cutting all the mortice holes out. Follow the advice on page 101 and don't forget you should aim to remove an even layer of chips with each pass of the chisel. If possible, stand 'in line' with the work so that you are always cutting at 90°. Your position will give you a continual visual check that this is happening.

7 Before you cut the tenons you need to cut the groove along the inside edges of all the rails and panel dividers, and on the edges of the corner posts, that will eventually house the panels. (It is much easier to do this on a complete piece of timber rather than after various bits have been cut off.) There are 2 ways of cutting these grooves:
i The traditional tool to use is a plough plane which comes complete with a range of different width cutters (see page 102). Whether you buy or borrow one of these, if you have never used one before make sure you practise on plenty of waste wood first and follow the advice I have given for success with this tool. If you are unfortunate enough to have a piece of very cross-grained wood, set a mortice gauge to the width of the groove and 'trail' the two points along the line of the groove first to give the plough plane a start and prevent the timber from tearing.
ii If you have, or can borrow, an electric router (see page 98) this job will be much easier. However, you should clamp an extra length of wood in the vice alongside each rail to give the machine extra width to work on. Fit a routing bit of the appropriate width, set the fence and away you go.

8 Once the grooves have been cut, cut out the tenons as described on page 101. Then assemble all the frames dry to check that everything fits. *Don't* glue anything yet.

9 The frames having been completed you can now turn your attention to the panels. As these take no structural strain the pine boards that form them can simply be glued together (a rub joint – see page 103). Cut the timber to length score the edges to be glued with a marking knife, apply glue and use sash cramps to hold the panel together till the glue has cured (dried).

When all 8 panels have been made (note that the 2 centre panels on the front and back are the same size as the end panels but that the remaining 4 are slightly narrower), you will need to remove all traces of glue with a sharp smoothing plane (see page 105).

10 Now 'square up' each panel using a steel rule and carpenter's square and a pencil, but don't trim it to its final size yet. Always allow extra length and width. Mark out in pencil the area you want to be 'raised' in the centre of the panel.

Raised fielded panels are not too difficult to cut providing that you start the right way. Once you have pencilled in the portion to be raised you need to cut away the timber immediately surrounding it. This can be done using a variety of tools: a plough plane, rebate plane or electric router.

If you decide to use a plough plane, select a fairly wide cutter and make a start by ploughing a groove along the pencil lines you have drawn (see page 102). This should be fairly easy when you are working *with* the grain. However, working across the grain raises problems and here it is best to score a very deep line with a marking knife first and to re-score the line as the plough plane removes shavings. This will ensure that no 'break out' of the end grain occurs. You should also lower the little spur cutter in the plough plane sole. (The purpose of this spur is to cut the fibres of the wood just before the cutter comes along. This is designed to prevent the wood from tearing, but theory and practice sometimes differ and in reality the spur may be fairly ineffective.)

Once you have ploughed around all 4 sides of each centre portion, you will be left with the raised section in the middle, a groove and a great deal of waste wood on the outside to be removed. This is best planed off with a sharp jack plane (see page 98). The jack plane has a longer sole than the smoothing plane and it will therefore 'true' the surfaces much better. It is always worth both time and effort to remove the plane blade regularly and re-sharpen it on the oilstone. A really sharp plane is a joy to use and you can even hear the difference. The shavings come off with a whistle!

Personally, however, I must admit to a great enthusiasm for the electric router. It will cut the initial groove very

quickly, and if you move the fence on the machine, it will also take off the waste wood on the outside too.

Perhaps the most awkward job of all when working on a panel is holding it still while you work. I use two cramps that have nylon heads and they work quite well, but the panel still moves, especially if you are putting on pressure with a plough plane. Consequently, you must re-adjust the panel continually as you work. It takes a good deal of patience to cut the panels, but at the end they will look simply beautiful.

11 Now take one of your assembled frameworks for the front or back. Mark or pencil in letters on the inside edges of each joint to show which fits which. Take off the top rail and fit the centre panel in place. This will require a further planing off around the edges of the panel so that it will slide in neatly. Ideally you should aim to get the panel to fit, but make sure it still has room in the grooves to expand and contract slightly.

Next fit the 2 outer panels and put the top rail back on. This represents one side of the cabinet. Repeat this procedure for the other side, then fit the end rails and end panels in place.

12 Using a smoothing plane, work over each rail to 'clean up' the wood. Fit the sash cramps in position on the assembled chest and check that everything fits and is square (see page 23, step 6).

On such a large and complex job it is best to glue only one section together at a time. My method is:
i Glue together the front panel and corner posts, then the back panel and corner posts;
ii When the glue has cured, remove the cramps from these panels and clean off any glue residue;
iii Glue and cramp the ends in place. Check that the chest is square before tightening up the cramps. If it isn't, slacken off the cramps and re-arrange them so that the heads pull off-centre so lifting the cramp slightly off the chest at one end. This should pull the chest back into square.

Glueing up the chest this way, rather than all at once, will alleviate dealing with lots of cramps and seemingly dozens of little wood blocks that persist in falling out of the cramp heads.

The base
Traditionally, the base for the chest would also have been framed and panelled, but to simplify the job I elected to use tongue-and-groove panelling.

1 Cut out and glue in position inside the chest the 4 battens of wood which will support the base. You'll need to use G cramps to hold these in place whilst the glue cures.

2 Cut the tongue-and-groove boards to length to fit across the short dimension of the chest. Then cut notches in the outer corners of the end boards to accommodate the corner posts.

3 Now fit the boards in place, working from the ends towards the middle. (You'll need someone to help you here.) You will find that the boards can be flexed to form an arch allowing you to slot the centre piece in position and once the boards rest on the supporting battens, the slack is taken up and they should all lie flat. However, some patience and a calm assistant are essential!

The lid
The lid is a little more traditional in design than the base but still makes use of tongue-and-groove panelling.

1 Cut the side, end and centre rails to length and mark out the mortice and tenon joints as described above. Cut out all the joints and fit the framework together dry as you did for the sides of the chest to ensure everything fits.

2 You now need to cut a rebate (see page 98) around the inside edges of all the rails on what will eventually be the underside of the lid. The tongue-and-groove boards have to fit into this rebate.

Take the frame apart and mark carefully in pencil the area to be cut away. Then use a marking knife and gauge to score in the lines, and finally remove the waste wood as you did for the raised and fielded panels (see step 10).

3 Clean up all the timber with a sharp smoothing plane and then glue and cramp the frame together as described above.

4 Cut your panelling to length and check that the boards fit snugly into the rebate you have cut on the underside of the lid. You may need to cut away a tongue from the ends.

When you are happy with the fit, glue the boards into the rebate.

5 A chest of this quality must have at least 3 proper brass hinges to hold the lid in place. A rebate for each has to be cut into the top rail of the chest to the full depth of the hinge flaps. This will then allow the lid to open fully and pass the vertical before being 'stayed' with a brass cabinet stay.

Using a marking gauge, scribe the depth of the hinges onto the top rail and then, using a chisel, very carefully remove the wood to allow the hinge to fit flush. Don't rush this job and only remove a very light quantity of wood at each pass. Careful marking out is the key. Don't be afraid to scribe very deeply around the area where the rebates for the hinges go. Hold the chisel very firmly and be sure to control the

cuts you are making. The rail you are working on is not very wide and any slip now will spoil the finished chest.

Once the rebates for the hinges are cut, position the hinges and temporarily screw them into place (2 screws only in each hinge). Position the lid onto the top and get the overhangs equal on all sides. Once you are sure of the position, mark on the underside of the lid exactly where the other hinge flaps should go. Unscrew the hinges from the chest and screw them onto the lid. Now replace the lid, fitting the hinges back into the rebates you have cut and screw in all the

screws. This procedure sounds lengthy, but it works.

Note: always drill pilot holes for the hinge screws. Remember that brass screws are very soft and will easily break off in the wood. If you find any resistance as you drive the screw in, don't force it. Remove the screw, drill the pilot hole a fraction deeper, and rub the screw with a lump of candlewax – this will keep you out of trouble.

Finally, fit a brass cabinet stay to prevent the lid from straining the hinges when it is open. These stays can be found in good ironmongers, but not

usually in the big DIY chain stores.

The lid should now fit perfectly and will forever hold in that beautiful scent of pine. Having put so much work into the chest don't skimp on the finishing-off stage. Glasspaper all the wood lovingly and then apply several layers of beeswax polish, buffing up the finish with a soft cloth between each layer. If you polish it regularly you will gradually build up that lovely soft shine which is so attractive with pine.

I always leave a shaving or two in the box – for posterity!!

Cutting list

Corner post	4 off	508 × 64 × 64mm (20 × 2½ × 2½in)	Timber
Side rail	4 off	1041 × 64 × 22mm (41 × 2½ × ⅞in)	Timber
Vertical panel divider	4 off	422 × 64 × 22mm (16⅝ × 2½ × ⅞in)	Timber
End rail	4 off	483 × 64 × 22mm (19 × 2½ × ⅞in)	Timber
Panelling	28 off	359 × 121 × 16mm (14⅛ × 4¾ × ⅝in)	Timber
Lid side rail	2 off	1162 × 89 × 22mm (45¾ × 3½ × ⅞in)	Timber
end rail	2 off	502 × 89 × 22mm (19¾ × 3½ × ⅞in)	Timber
centre rail	1 off	502 × 64 × 22mm (19¾ × 2½ × ⅞in)	Timber
infill	11 off	449 × 89 × 16mm (17¾ × 3½ × ⅝in)	Tongue-and-groove boarding
Base support	2 off	964 × 47 × 22mm (38 × 1⅞ × ⅞in)	Timber
	2 off	405 × 47 × 22mm (16 × 1⅞ × ⅞in)	Timber
Base	12 off	489 × 89 × 16mm (19¼ × 3½ × ⅝in)	Tongue-and-groove boarding

Ancillaries

	3 off	76mm (3in) × 20mm (¾in) brass hinges
	1 off	203mm (8in) brass cabinet stay

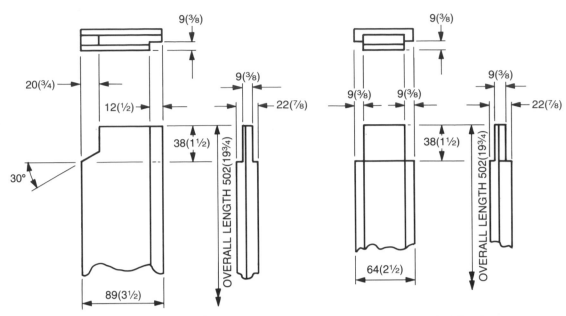

LID END CROSS MEMBERS
MAKE 2

LID CENTRE CROSS RAIL

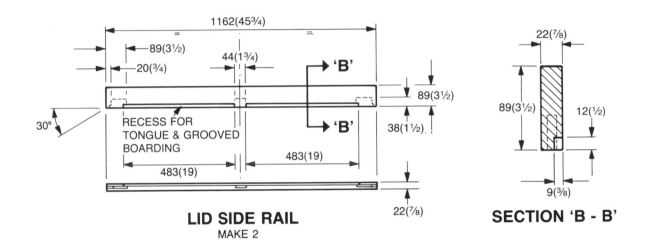

LID SIDE RAIL
MAKE 2

RECESS FOR
TONGUE & GROOVED
BOARDING

SECTION 'B - B'

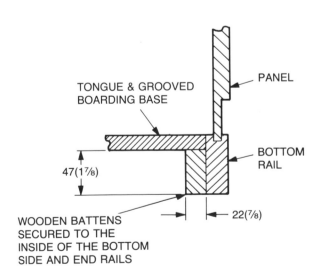

TONGUE & GROOVED
BOARDING BASE

PANEL

BOTTOM
RAIL

WOODEN BATTENS
SECURED TO THE
INSIDE OF THE BOTTOM
SIDE AND END RAILS

**Section through
chest bottom rail to
illustrate method of
securing tongue and
grooved base**

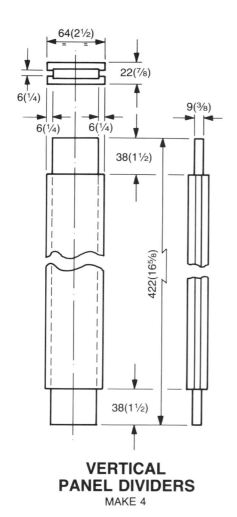

**VERTICAL
PANEL DIVIDERS**
MAKE 4

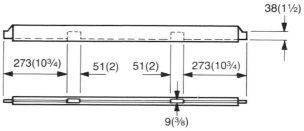

**Detail for mortice for panel dividers in top rails
Corresponding mortice also required in bottom rail**

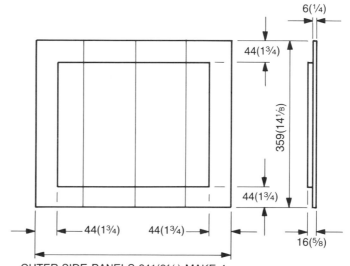

OUTER SIDE PANELS 241(9½) MAKE 4
CENTRAL SIDE PANELS 394(15½) MAKE 2
END PANELS 419(16½) MAKE 2

PANELLING

FABRICATE BY BUTTING AND GLUING
121(4¾) × 16(⅝) THICK STRIPS

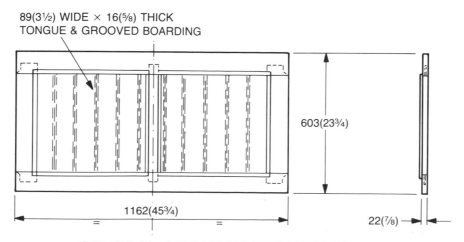

89(3½) WIDE × 16(⅝) THICK
TONGUE & GROOVED BOARDING

GENERAL ARRANGEMENT OF LID

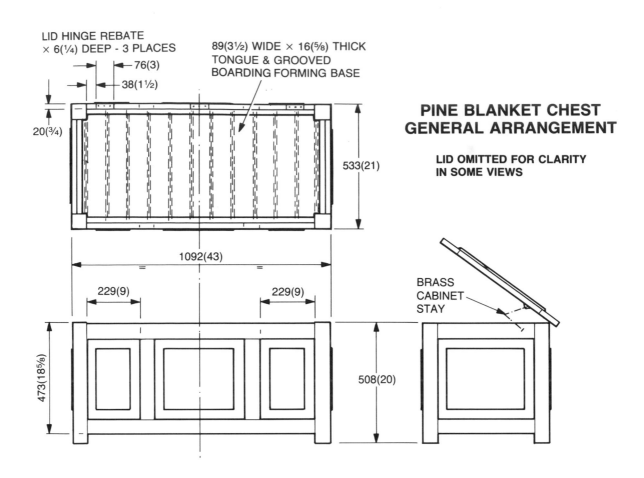

LID HINGE REBATE
× 6(¼) DEEP - 3 PLACES

76(3)

38(1½)

20(¾)

89(3½) WIDE × 16(⅝) THICK
TONGUE & GROOVED
BOARDING FORMING BASE

PINE BLANKET CHEST
GENERAL ARRANGEMENT

LID OMITTED FOR CLARITY
IN SOME VIEWS

533(21)

1092(43)

229(9)

229(9)

473(18⅝)

508(20)

BRASS
CABINET
STAY

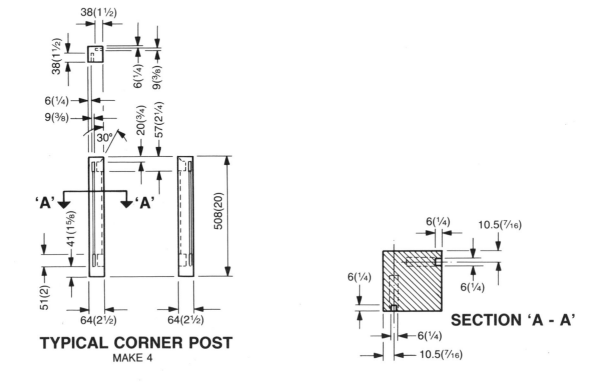

38(1½)

38(1½)

6(¼)

9(⅜)

6(¼)

9(⅜)

30°

20(¾)

57(2¼)

'A'   'A'

508(20)

41(1⅝)

51(2)

64(2½)

64(2½)

TYPICAL CORNER POST
MAKE 4

6(¼)   10.5(⁷⁄₁₆)

6(¼)

6(¼)

6(¼)

10.5(⁷⁄₁₆)

SECTION 'A - A'

Free-standing shelving unit

Trimming the top of the kitchen cupboard using a plane

Cutting grooves with an electric router

Using a belt sander to even out planks

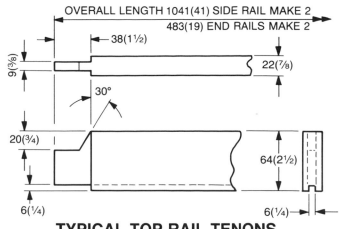

OVERALL LENGTH 1041(41) SIDE RAIL MAKE 2
483(19) END RAILS MAKE 2
38(1½)
9(⅜)
22(⅞)
30°
20(¾)
64(2½)
6(¼)
6(¼)

TYPICAL TOP RAIL TENONS

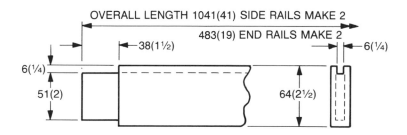

OVERALL LENGTH 1041(41) SIDE RAILS MAKE 2
483(19) END RAILS MAKE 2
38(1½)
6(¼)
6(¼)
51(2)
64(2½)

TYPICAL BOTTOM RAIL TENONS

PLAN VIEW OF RAIL AS PER TOP RAIL
SEE PAGE   FOR DETAILS OF BATTEN
SUPPORTING TONGUE & GROOVED
BOARDING BASE

TABLE AND BENCHES

These two basic table designs have a great deal in common. At first glance they look very different, but the legs and rails are constructed in exactly the same way. What's more, the benches have the same construction too. One table and its benches are topped with traditional pine, while the other has a black ash melamine-faced man-made board top with a Nordic Redwood surround. The legs of the black ash table and benches have a decorative groove running along their outer edges.

In addition to the long benches for the sides, the all-pine table has end benches and accommodates six people. End benches for the other table can be made if you wish as the joints used are identical. Once you have mastered the jointing techniques required, it is just a case of choosing which style, or indeed colour, table top will best fit your home.

I Start by marking out the legs and rails. Don't be tempted to mark out just one, cut it out and then go on to the next. Mark out *all* of them together. If you clamp the 4 pieces of timber for the legs together when you mark the initial pencil lines and then do the same for the 2 sets of rails, you can be certain that they will all be the right length.

Now mark the face side and face edge of each leg and rail (see page 99). These marks will give you a 'datum line' from which you can set your marking gauge (see page 99) for all the other measurements.

Take the clamps off the legs and, working from each face side and face edge mark, take the initial pencil lines all round the pieces of timber using a carpenter's square (see page 99).

2 The joints which will hold the legs and rails together are haunched mortice and tenon joints (see page 101). The reason for using this joint is to stop the rail from twisting and so give greater rigidity to the table. If the tenons were left 'un-haunched' and therefore the same width as the rail, you would have to cut away so much wood inside the leg to accommodate them that the joint would not be very strong. So a step is cut (see plans) making the width and depth of most of the tenon less than that of the rail. As the table top sits on top of the legs and conceals this joint, there is no need to have an angled haunch, as you do for the blanket chest (see pages 52 and 55).

The mortice slots are very deep and actually meet inside the leg. Therefore you also have to cut a 45° mitre off the end of each tenon so that the 2 tenons fit at right angles in the middle of the leg.

3 When each finished tenon is pushed fully into the mortice, the tenon's shoulders should be flush onto the leg. If not, check very carefully for the gauge lines. Usually you will find that you have not quite removed all the waste wood. Take the tenon out of the mortice and, using a large bevel-edged chisel, trim off the waste. Re-fit the tenon and if it still does not fit, check that it is not too long for the mortice hole and that all chippings are out of the hole. A little patience is perhaps the best tool in any

workshop – especially when cutting joints. And believe me – practice really does make perfect!

Once all the mortices and tenons have been cut to your satisfaction, fit the legs and rails together 'dry' (i.e. without glue) and see if everything fits. This is a sort of woodworker's 'dress rehearsal' for the big day.

4 Now pencil in the mortice holes on the inside of the rails into which the 'buttons' for fixing the table top will slot. Treble check that all the markings are on the inside edges! There could be nothing more frustrating than a row of slots on the outside edge of your table. When you are sure you have marked them all in correctly, knife the pencil lines in and then cut out all the slots.

Next cut out all the buttons using a tenon saw. Note that you need 16 Type A buttons for the all-pine version, and 10 Type B and 6 Type C for the black ash version (see plans). These are a very simple but efficient method of attachment, and they also have another purpose: to allow the top to 'move' on the framework, but still keep it flat. I usually mark them out on a long batten of wood and cut them out together – mass production!

5 Once all the pieces of timber and joints have been cut and a successful dry run achieved, mark in pencil a letter or number on each tenon peg and on the inside of each corresponding mortice hole. These pencil marks should not be removed as they will help you assemble the joints again after the 'cleaning up' operation.

Now completely dismantle the framework, sharpen up your smoothing plane (see page 105) and, with a very small set (thin shaving), work over all the timber removing all visible pencil lines, gauge marks, etc. This cleaning up before the glueing stage is vital and will save many hours of work later.

6 Ideally you should use sash cramps (see page 103) when glueing the framework together. These can be bought or hired, but a cheaper alternative is to buy cramp heads and fit them onto stout battens of wood.

Before glueing, set out everything

tidily in your workshop or garage – cramps ready and blocks of wood to prevent the metal heads damaging the timber. Apply glue to all the joints following the manufacturer's instructions carefully. It is a good idea to apply glue to all the tenons and shoulders first, then the mortice holes and work methodically so that you don't miss any out.

Now assemble the rails into the legs and cramp them in position. It is wonderful to have an assistant (who doesn't talk too much) to help hold the cramps and position the waste blocks of wood behind the cramp heads. You can do this by yourself, but it is more difficult. Once the table is all cramped up, take a long batten of wood and check across the diagonals of the frame that it is 'square' (see page 23, step 6). If you find that it is out of square, slacken off the cramps and check that you have them pulling evenly on each corner. Tighten up and check the diagonals again with the batten of wood. If all is well, leave for the glue to cure.

Whichever table you decide to make, the procedure is identical up until this stage. The same applies to the benches.

The bench framework
The benches are constructed using the same joints and method as for the table. The only difference is the dimensions. Decide at the outset how many of each size of bench you want to make so that you can mark out all the legs and rails together. The bench legs are not as heavy in section as the table legs but they are very sturdy.

Pine table and bench tops
For the traditional table I used Nordic red pine throughout. The legs do not show too much, but for the top it is essential to have a wood that both finishes easily and looks good. The top of a table is large and prominent and a poor finish will spoil the whole job.

A variety of thicknesses and widths of ready-prepared pine are available at most good timber merchants. Selecting the wood for the top is important so don't arrive at a busy merchant at dawn on a Monday morning! Mid-afternoon is better – then most of the builders are well out of the way, and the staff have more time to assist you. 'Eye' each board carefully and avoid anything that is twisted or bent. I don't mind knots – after all, trees do have branches – but make sure that the knot is firm and won't fall out. I always ask to see what's available, and I volunteer to put the stack

back as I find it. Wear industrial gloves as turning timber over is a hard job and large splinters are always lurking for the unprepared. I always buy an extra board in case of 'mishaps'. If I don't use it, I have one in store for the next job.

1 Once back in the workshop with your boards make a further examination of your purchase. Decide which planks will look best on the table and bench tops. Sometimes you can match up the grain nicely. Also, arrange the planks so that the growth rings on the ends of the boards go in opposite directions. This will help to compensate for any movement in the table top (see page 103). Remember that wood lives. We can't stop it moving so we must compensate, and arranging the planks in this way will help. When you are happy with your arrangement, cut the planks to length.

2 Once the planks have been sorted, decide how you intend to join them together. Nowadays you can simply use glue and nothing else. Technical advances have taken us a long way from the old carpenter's glue pot bubbling on the tortoise stove and the pungent smell that surrounded it. The new PVA glues are much easier to use. They come ready mixed, involve far less waste and, perhaps most important, are very strong. The most commonly used glue in the UK, Evo-stick Resin W, is in fact stronger than wood itself. If you glue together two offcuts of wood, cramp them together and try to separate them after 24 hours you will find the wood grain breaks first, not the glue line.

Personally, however, I like to use dowel joints between planks as well as glue. This joint is fairly easy, and as it creates an even greater glueing area it makes for a stronger joint.

3 If you decide to join the planks with dowels as well as glue, cramp them together with G cramps so that the edges are all together (page 103). Using a square, mark out the position for the dowel rod holes. Marking out in this way is essential, otherwise the holes and dowels will not line up. Don't forget that with the 2 outer planks it is only the *inside* edges that need dowel rod holes! Separate the planks and bore the holes for the dowels at 90° in both planes (see page 103).

4 Cut all the dowel rods to length making sure that they are a little shorter than the combined depth of both holes, then apply glue and assemble the planks as explained on page 103. You will need

sash cramps to hold them together while the glue is curing. Not only do the sash cramps pull all the joints together, but the steel bar is a very useful flat surface on which the planks can rest while the glue dries.

When all the cramps have been fitted, place the whole assembly flat on the floor. Usually you will find that a plank will 'creep' up at one edge. Using a hammer and a waste block of wood, hammer the plank down. You may even have to loosen off one of the cramps to do this. You may find it an advantage to have 2 sash cramps on the top side, as this does help to keep the planks flat.

It is always advisable to allow 24 hours in a warm place for the glue to cure completely before removing the sash cramps. If you work in a shed or a garage, some heating must be provided or the glue will not cure properly.

5 After you have removed all the cramps, plane down and smooth off the top. However careful or accurate your glueing up is, you will always get one or two planks that are slightly proud (i.e. part of the plank is raised) and these have to be planed off. A very well-sharpened jack plane (see page 98) will do this job, but it needs a lot of skill to plane all over the top and remove even amounts of wood. An easier method is to use a belt sander (see page 105). These machines will work all over the top, sanding off any proud edges and removing the glue lines that inevitably show up between the planks. It is worth spending a good few hours on the top and getting a surface you will be proud to look at.

6 Once the sanding is done, round off the corners and chamfer the edges with a jack plane. Alternatively an electric router (see page 98) with the right cutter can produce a perfect rounded edge in minutes.

7 Now to fit the top to the legs. The easiest way to do this is to lay the top on the floor, top side down (put a suitable sheet or blanket underneath), and then to lay the leg-framework upside down on the underside of the top.

Fit the wooden buttons into the mortice holes that you cut on the inside of the rails and screw them to the table top using supascrews (see page 104). Check the length of screws you are going to use very carefully. There is nothing worse than a beautiful table with a line of screw points projecting through the top.

Fit the pine seats onto the benches using exactly the same procedure.

Man-made board and timber-topped table and benches

Although the construction of the leg framework for this table and benches is identical to the pine version, you can produce an entirely different look by cutting a routed line along both edges of the face sides of the legs and rails. An electric router fitted with a fence and a 'V' cutter will do this shaping job very quickly. However, if you don't have one I suggest using a plough plane (see page 102) to cut the grooves and a chisel to finish them off.

I used two different methods to joint the pine surrounds to the man-made board for the tops. On the benches the surrounds are butt-jointed, and on the top they are mitred. It doesn't matter which you use – it's really a question of personal taste. The butt joint is simpler, but I think the mitre looks better.

I Start by selecting your melamine-faced board. I chose black ash but there is a wide choice of other colours and it is usually available in ideal widths for the top and benches so that the only cutting required is to length. Pencil in the line you intend to cut along and use one of the saws suggested on page 98 for cutting melamine-faced board successfully.

2 Having cut the board for the top and benches to length, you should now make the surrounds.

To get the surrounds flush with the top, you need to cut a rebate to a depth equal to the thickness of the melamine-faced board. The rebate also has to be of sufficient width to get a good fixing on both table and bench tops. A rebate plane or the ever-faithful router will cut this joint very satisfactorily (see page 98). It is probably best to get a feel of the job on the bench tops first – they are smaller, and the butt joint is less complicated.

Quite often, cutting the rebate is not the problem. Holding the wood steady is. A useful tip is to start with a wider plank than you need which is easier to fix in your vice or work bench. You can then cut the rebate on the edge and saw off the excess width. If you cut the edging to size first, it will be rather narrow and so far more difficult to hold.

3 Once the rebates have been cut on all 4 edging pieces, offer them up to the melamine top to ensure the depth is correct. Now pencil in the areas that have to be cut away from the inner edges of both end pieces (see plans). Double check that you have marked these on the right pieces before you cut them off. Drill the holes for the fixing screws as shown on the plans and then glue and screw the bench top framework together.

Once the glue has cured, glue and screw the board in place from underneath. Ordinary PVA glue will fix the edges of the board to the wooden frame but won't adhere to the melamine facing. However it does provide a very good (dare I say it?) gap-filler and will neatly occupy any slight crevices between the frame and the melamine-faced board. This is important as gaps at the edges would be a trap for dust and

dirt – the very last thing you want with a table.

A word of caution here – again, be very careful about the length of screw you use. Melamine-faced board has a high gloss surface, and a screw point – even just below the surface – will show. This is because the screw starts to force the chips in the board upwards and so a bump appears. You will find that the new Supascrews with double threads (see page 104) will get a much better grip in the chipboard than the traditional screw thread.

4 Having gained some experience with the benches, you should be ready to tackle the table top frame. Cut the rebates on all 4 pieces of timber as explained above and use a sliding bevel gauge to mark in pencil the 45° mitre at each corner (see page 102). Then use a marking knife to etch in the cutting line round the wood. Use a very sharp tenon saw and mitre block to cut the mitres. As you finish each side of the frame, clamp it to the melamine top to ensure everything fits together properly. If any of the mitres are slightly out, use a very sharp plane to take off just one shaving at a time. Be very patient and keep checking the fit, otherwise you will get 'gappy' mitres which look very untidy. Once successful mitring has been achieved (words make it sound so easy!), glue the framework together, and then glue and screw the melamine board in place as explained above for the bench tops.

5 Finally, fix the tops of the benches and table to their frameworks using wooden buttons and screws as explained for the pine-topped version (see page 58, step 7).

Do make sure you spend plenty of time glasspapering and varnishing or polishing the finished furniture. After all that effort you really shouldn't spoil the effect by skimping on the finishing off!

Cutting list

Pine table

Side rails	2 off	1302 × 108 × 27mm (51¼ × 4¼ × 1⅛in)	Timber
End rails	2 off	654 × 108 × 27mm (25¾ × 4¼ × 1⅛in)	Timber
Legs	4 off	762 × 76 × 70mm (30 × 3 × 2¾in)	Timber
Table top	4 off	1588 × 194 × 22mm (62½ × 7⅝ × ⅞in)	Timber
Buttons 'A'	Make from 900 × 35 × 25mm (36 × 1⅜ × 1in)		Timber
Dowels	Make from 3750mm (150in) × 9mm (⅜in) diam dowel		

Black ash-topped table

Side rails	2 off	1302 × 108 × 27mm (51¼ × 4¼ × 1⅛in)	Timber
End rails	2 off	654 × 108 × 27mm (25¾ × 4¼ × 1⅛in)	Timber
Legs	4 off	762 × 76 × 70mm (30 × 3 × 2¾in)	Timber
Table top frame	2 off	1588 × 95 × 32mm (62½ × 3¾ × 1¼in)	Timber
	2 off	743 × 95 × 32mm (29¼ × 3¾ × 1¼in)	Timber
Inset	1 off	1448 × 603 × 16mm (57 × 22¾ × ⅝in)	Man-made board
Buttons 'B'	Make from 440 × 35 × 25mm (17½ × 1⅜ × 1in)		Timber
Buttons 'C'	Make from 375 × 41 × 35mm (15 × 1⅝ × 1⅜in)		Timber
Plugs	Make from 38mm (1½in) × 12mm (½in) diam dowel		

Pine bench

Side rails	2 off	997 × 108 × 27mm (39¼ × 4¼ × 1⅛in)	Timber
End rails	2 off	311 × 108 × 27mm (12¼ × 4¼ × 1⅛in)	Timber
Legs	4 off	441 × 64 × 64mm (17⅜ × 2½ × 2½in)	Timber
Bench top	2 off	1118 × 194 × 22mm (44 × 7⅝ × ⅞in)	Timber
Buttons 'A'	Make from 560 × 35 × 25mm (22½ × 1⅜ × 1in)		Timber
Dowels	Make from 870mm (34⅜in) × 9mm (⅜in) diam dowel		

Cutting list

Pine stool

Side rails	2 off	375 × 108 × 27mm (14¾ × 4¼ × 1⅛in)	Timber
End rails	2 off	311 × 108 × 27mm (12¼ × 4¼ × 1⅛in)	Timber
Legs	4 off	441 × 64 × 64mm (17⅜ × 2½ × 2½in)	Timber
Stool top	2 off	508 × 194 × 22mm (20 × 7⅝ × ⅞in)	Timber
Buttons 'A'	Make from 460 × 35 × 25mm (18 × 1⅜ × 1in)		Timber
Dowels	Make from 390mm (15⅜in) × 9mm (⅜in) diam dowel		

Black ash-topped bench

Side rails	2 off	997 × 108 × 27mm (39¼ × 4¼ × 1⅛in)	Timber
End rails	2 off	311 × 108 × 27mm (12¼ × 4¼ × 1⅛in)	Timber
Legs	4 off	441 × 64 × 64mm (17⅜ × 2½ × 2½in)	Timber
Bench top frame	2 off	1118 × 54 × 28mm (44 × 2⅛ × 1⅛in)	Timber
	2 off	381 × 54 × 28mm (15 × 2⅛ × 1⅛in)	Timber
Inset	1 off	1042 × 305 × 16mm (41 × 12 × ⅝in)	Man-made board
Buttons 'C'	Make from 630 × 41 × 35mm (25 × 1⅝ × 1⅜in)		Timber
Plugs	Make from 38mm (1½in) × 12mm (½in) diam dowel		

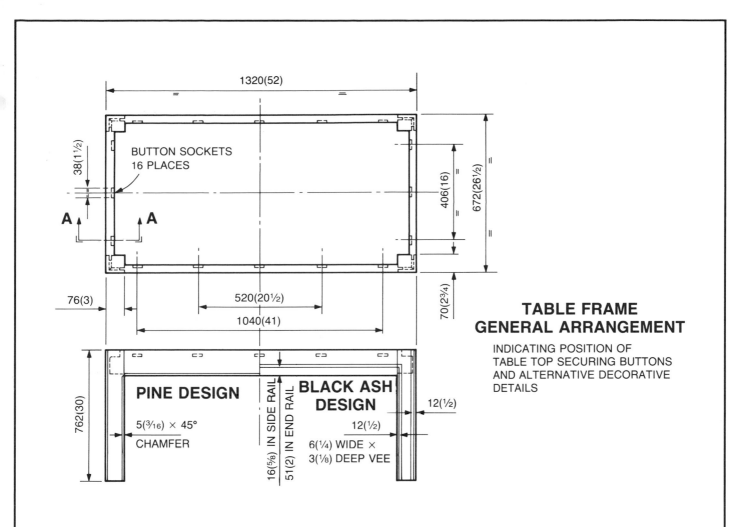

1320(52)

BUTTON SOCKETS
16 PLACES

38(1½)

406(16)

672(26½)

A

A

76(3)

520(20½)

1040(41)

70(2¾)

TABLE FRAME
GENERAL ARRANGEMENT

INDICATING POSITION OF
TABLE TOP SECURING BUTTONS
AND ALTERNATIVE DECORATIVE
DETAILS

762(30)

PINE DESIGN

5(³⁄₁₆) × 45°
CHAMFER

16(⅝) IN SIDE RAIL
51(2) IN END RAIL

**BLACK ASH
DESIGN**

6(¼) WIDE ×
3(⅛) DEEP VEE

12(½)

12(½)

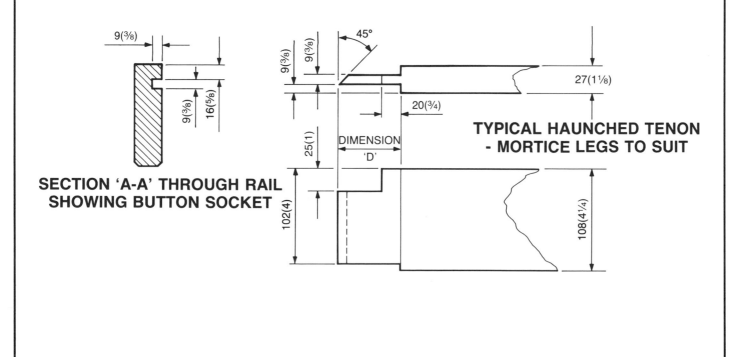

9(³⁄₈)

9(³⁄₈)

16(⅝)

SECTION 'A-A' THROUGH RAIL
SHOWING BUTTON SOCKET

45°

9(³⁄₈)

9(³⁄₈)

27(1⅛)

20(¾)

25(1)

DIMENSION
'D'

TYPICAL HAUNCHED TENON
- MORTICE LEGS TO SUIT

102(4)

108(4¼)

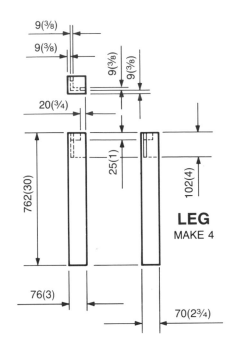

LEG
MAKE 4

9(³⁄₈)
9(³⁄₈)
9(³⁄₈)
9(³⁄₈)
20(³⁄₄)
25(1)
762(30)
102(4)
76(3)
70(2³⁄₄)

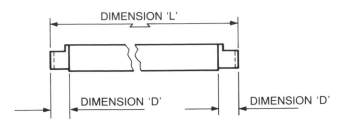

DIMENSION 'L'
DIMENSION 'D'
DIMENSION 'D'

RAILS - MAKE FROM 108(4¼) × 27(1⅛) TIMBER
SEE GENERAL ARRANGEMENT FOR BUTTON SOCKET POSITIONS

	DIMENSION L	DIMENSION D
SIDE RAILS MAKE 2	1302(51¼)	67(2⅝)
END RAILS MAKE 2	654(25¾)	60(2⅜)

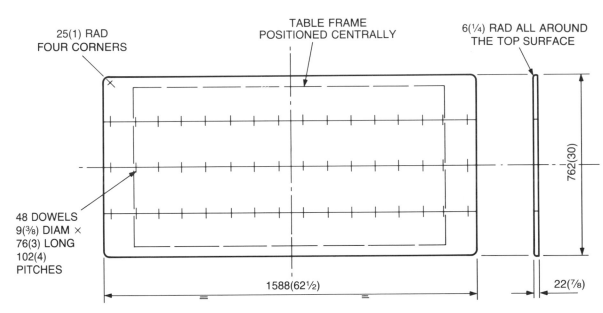

25(1) RAD
FOUR CORNERS

TABLE FRAME
POSITIONED CENTRALLY

6(¼) RAD ALL AROUND
THE TOP SURFACE

48 DOWELS
9(³⁄₈) DIAM ×
76(3) LONG
102(4)
PITCHES

762(30)

1588(62½)

22(⅞)

PINE TABLE TOP   MAKE WITH 194(7⅝) × 22(⅞) PLANKS

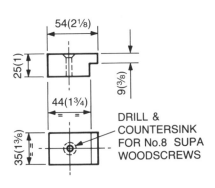

54(2⅛)
25(1)
9(³⁄₈)
44(1¾)
35(1³⁄₈)

DRILL &
COUNTERSINK
FOR No.8 SUPA
WOODSCREWS

TYPE 'A' BUTTONS
FOR PINE
TABLE TOP MAKE 16

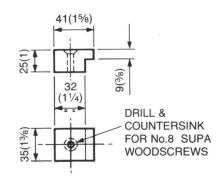

41(1⅝)
25(1)
9(³⁄₈)
32
(1¼)
35(1³⁄₈)

DRILL &
COUNTERSINK
FOR No.8 SUPA
WOODSCREWS

TYPE 'B' BUTTONS
FOR BLACK ASH TABLE TOP FOR
SIDE RAIL FIXING MAKE 10

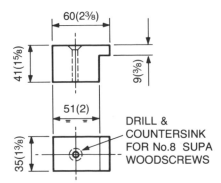

60(2⅜)
41(1⅝)
9(³⁄₈)
51(2)
35(1³⁄₈)

DRILL &
COUNTERSINK
FOR No.8 SUPA
WOODSCREWS

TYPE 'C' BUTTONS
FOR BLACK ASH TABLE TOP FOR
END RAIL FIXING MAKE 6

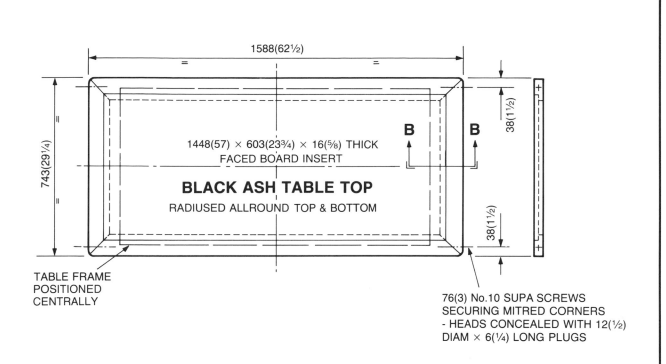

1588(62½)

743(29¼)

38(1½)

38(1½)

1448(57) × 603(23¾) × 16(⅝) THICK
FACED BOARD INSERT

BLACK ASH TABLE TOP
RADIUSED ALLROUND TOP & BOTTOM

B   B

TABLE FRAME
POSITIONED
CENTRALLY

76(3) No.10 SUPA SCREWS
SECURING MITRED CORNERS
- HEADS CONCEALED WITH 12(½)
DIAM × 6(¼) LONG PLUGS

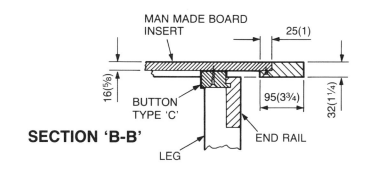

MAN MADE BOARD
INSERT

25(1)

16(⅝)

BUTTON
TYPE 'C'

95(3¾)

32(1¼)

SECTION 'B-B'

LEG

END RAIL

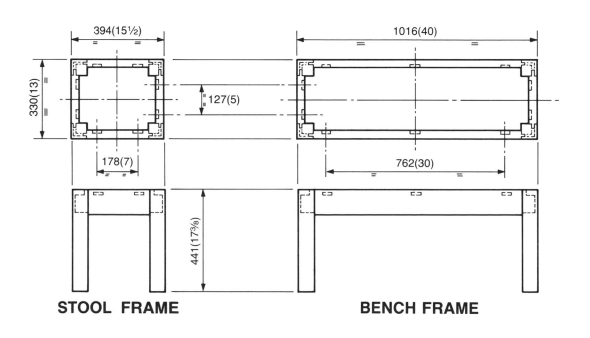

394(15½)

1016(40)

330(13)

127(5)

178(7)

762(30)

441(17⅜)

STOOL FRAME

BENCH FRAME

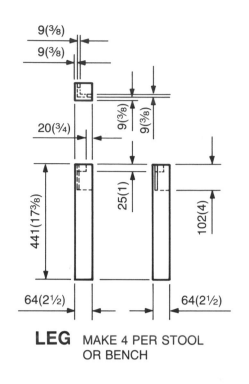

LEG MAKE 4 PER STOOL
OR BENCH

Legs & Rails to have decorative details as associated table

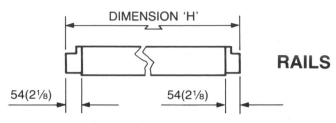

RAILS

MAKE FROM 108(4¼) × 27(1⅛) TIMBER
FOR REMAINING TENON DIMENSIONS SEE TABLE
TYPICAL HAUNCHED TENON DETAIL
GENERAL FRAME ARRANGEMENTS ABOVE GIVE
BUTTON POCKET POSITIONS - OTHER DETAILS AS
PER SECTION 'A - A' OF TABLE DRAWING - ALL
SOCKET 38(1½) LONG

	DIMENSION 'H'
STOOL SIDE RAIL	375(14¾)
BENCH SIDE RAIL	997(39¼)
STOOL & BENCH END RAILS	311(12¼)

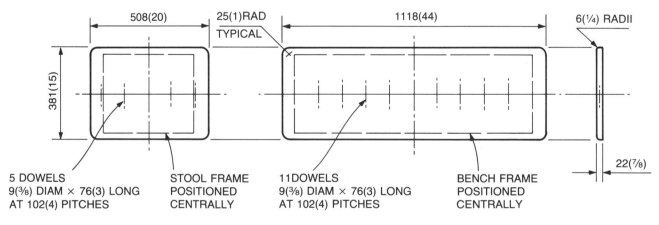

5 DOWELS
9(⅜) DIAM × 76(3) LONG
AT 102(4) PITCHES

STOOL FRAME
POSITIONED
CENTRALLY

11 DOWELS
9(⅜) DIAM × 76(3) LONG
AT 102(4) PITCHES

BENCH FRAME
POSITIONED
CENTRALLY

PINE STOOL TOP

MAKE WITH 194(7⅝) × 22(⅞) PLANKS
8 OFF TYPE 'A' BUTTONS REQUIRED

PINE BENCH TOP

MAKE WITH 194(7⅝) × 22(⅞) PLANKS
10 OFF TYPE 'A' BUTTONS REQUIRED

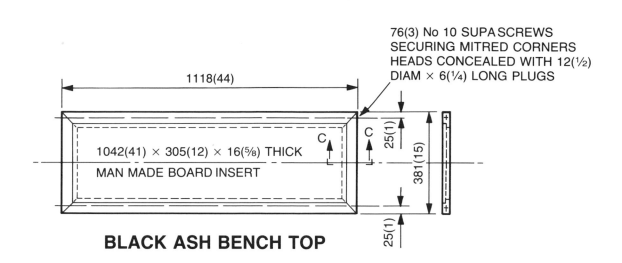

76(3) No 10 SUPA SCREWS
SECURING MITRED CORNERS
HEADS CONCEALED WITH 12(½)
DIAM × 6(¼) LONG PLUGS

1118(44)

1042(41) × 305(12) × 16(⅝) THICK
MAN MADE BOARD INSERT

25(1)

381(15)

25(1)

C C

BLACK ASH BENCH TOP

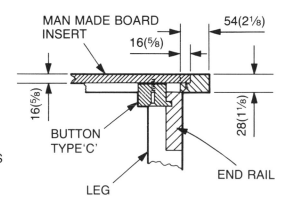

MAN MADE BOARD
INSERT

54(2⅛)

16(⅝)

16(⅝)

28(1⅛)

BUTTON
TYPE 'C'

LEG

END RAIL

10 OFF TYPE 'C' BUTTONS
REQUIRED TO SECURE
BLACK ASH BENCH TOP

SECTION C - C

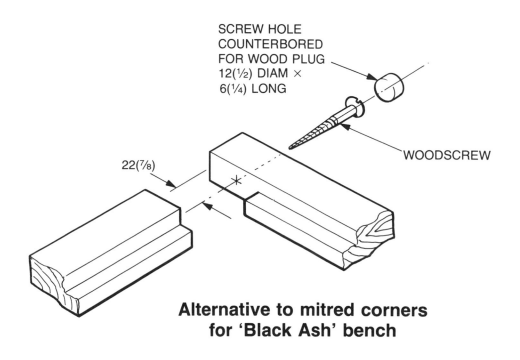

SCREW HOLE
COUNTERBORED
FOR WOOD PLUG
12(½) DIAM ×
6(¼) LONG

WOODSCREW

22(⅞)

Alternative to mitred corners
for 'Black Ash' bench

GARDEN BENCH

Anyone who has visited a garden centre recently cannot fail to be impressed at the vast range of plants and accessories that are available. None of the old fence posts anymore, but water pumps to create your own Niagara falls and huge green compost bins that look like lunar bugs instead. Little gnomes are out, but life-size stone Grecian ladies (who I am sure would shiver if left parked in my garden) are in. For those occasional Saturdays and Sundays when the sun does manage to shine, and you have time to sit back and admire your garden I have designed and built a garden bench and chair. An interesting feature is the folding shelf that will hold your coffee cup while you converse with the Grecian stone waitress at your elbow!

All the joints used in this project are traditional and sturdy, so this is a good piece to practise your skills on. The bench is a full 1.7m (6 feet) long, but if you want something shorter, just reduce the length of each piece, i.e. mark out all rails at, say, 1.2m (4 feet). As this has to stand out in all weathers, a good wood preservative is essential.

I would advise you to decide in advance whether you intend to make both the bench and the chair as this means you can work out your cutting list and get everything from the timber merchant at the same time. You will then be sure the wood matches and can also do all your marking out together.

As with all my projects there is room for you to adapt my design if it is not quite to your taste. So, for example, you may prefer to have all the uprights for the seat back the same height or to cut a different shape, or even none at all, in the central upright. It's up to you – but make sure you find time to sit in it once all the hard work is over!

1 As usual you should start by studying the plans carefully to familiarise yourself with the method of construction. The joints used are single or twin stopped mortice and tenons (see page 101). You will see that the front and rear legs and the bottom rails are made from wood of identical thickness. Therefore it is a good idea to mark out all the lengths you require, whether for just the bench or the bench and chair, together. Before you actually mark the lengths, however, decide which is going to be the face side and face edge of each piece. The most important thing to avoid is having a knot near a joint so you may need to 'juggle' your marking out to achieve this. Once you have marked out all the legs and bottom rails, cut them out.

2 Now cramp the front legs together and pencil in the position of the mortice holes for the seat rails and bottom rails using a carpenter's square (see page 101). Then uncramp, turn them and recramp to mark the position of the mortice holes for the front rail. Make sure you haven't marked any of these holes on your face side and face edges!

Go through the same procedure with the rear legs, marking the position of the bottom and seat rail mortices and those for the rear rail, the arm rests and the back support rail.

3 Cramp the bottom rails together and mark the shoulder lines for the twin tenons using a carpenter's square (see page 101). Uncramp them and continue the shoulder lines all the way round the wood. The reason for using twin tenons here is the width of the leg and rail. If you cut 1 huge mortice for a single tenon you would weaken the leg.

Set your mortice gauge to the required width for these and mark in both the tenons and the appropriate mortice holes as explained on page 101.

4 Lay out all the pieces on the garage or workshop floor and double check that you have marked everything correctly. 'Mentally' fit the pieces together and scribble over in pencil the areas to be cut away. (Anything is better than finding you have chopped a large hole on the wrong side of a leg!)

When you are sure you have marked everything correctly use a marking knife to score in your pencil lines and then you are ready to cut the joints out. Follow all the advice on page 101 for cutting twin mortice and tenons and do work with a really sharp saw and chisels.

5 Now cut the timber for the seat rails to length and clamp the pieces together. Pencil in the shoulder lines for the tenons, unclamp the rails and continue the shoulder lines round. Set your mortice gauge and mark in the width of the tenons and mortice holes.

Note that for the bench you also need 2 intermediate supports for the seat which differ from the outer seat rails only in length and the size of their tenons. Cut these to length now and mark out the tenons.

Cut out all the tenons on all the seat rails and the mortices in the front and rear legs.

Now mark out the identical curvature needed on top of all 4 seat rails (2 only for the chair). The ideal tool to use to cut away the waste is an electric jigsaw (see page 98) but if you do not have one use a coping saw (see page 101). Once the curve has been cut, remove the saw cuts with a spokeshave (page 105) – there really is no alternative to this most useful tool. However, don't work from one side right across to the other side. Work down each half from either end, stopping just before the middle. If you don't, you are likely to tear the wood.

6 Cut out the front and rear rails, which are identical.

Both rails require tenons at each end to slot into the mortice holes you have already pencilled in on the front and rear legs. As with all the joints on this project they are stopped, i.e. the mortice holes are not cut right through the wood so that the end of the tenon is hidden. They need to be as deep as they are in order to give rigidity to such a long bench.

Once you have marked and cut out the tenons and mortice holes for the ends, you need to mark and cut out the 2 mortice holes on the inside of each rail that will accommodate the 2 intermediate seat rails.

7 The top back rail has to support all the back slats and so needs to be another sturdy piece of timber. Cut it to length and then mark and cut out the tenons and the mortice holes in the top of the rear legs but do not cut them out until you have planed an angle on the inside edge of the rail against which the slats will rest. It is best to use a jack plane (see page 98) for this as the extra length of its sole will do the job more accurately than that of a shorter plane.

When you have done this, cut out the mortice and tenon joints.

Pine blanket chest

Pine table and benches

Pine and black ash table and benches

The author putting a universal woodworking machine through its paces: surface planing

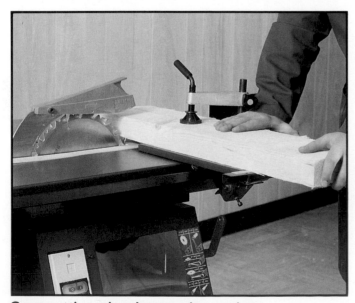

Cross-cutting using the tenoning carriage

Cutting slot mortice holes

8 With all the pieces and joints for the basic framework cut, sharpen your smoothing plane and work over all the timber to remove saw cuts, pencil lines, blemishes and so on. Assemble the bench or chair 'dry' to check that everything fits well.

9 The first part of the glueing operation is to glue each end together, i.e. a bottom rail, seat rail, front leg and rear leg. As the furniture will stand outside in all weathers it is vital to use a waterproof glue such as Cascamite One-shot available from builders' merchants. Avoid glues that are labelled 'water-resistant' – these are *not* suitable and will break down after only days out of doors.

Apply the glue to the joints and sash cramp each end frame together until the glue has cured.

10 Now you are ready to glue the front, rear, intermediate seat and top back rails in place. Have a dry run and then apply glue and cramp up. You may need to hire or borrow sash cramps with extending bars to achieve the length needed for the bench, and a patient assistant is also important. Working with long heavy sash cramps and lengthy pieces of timber is not easy.

11 After the glue has cured, remove all the cramps and, with a sharp chisel, cut away any glue residue around the joints. Do this carefully as any glue that is left visible will prevent the wood preservative from taking.

12 You now need to cut to length and fit the back support rail. This is a batten of wood that runs along the back of the seat onto which the bottom ends of the back slats are fixed. Before screwing it in position plane an angle along the inside edge corresponding to the one you cut on the top back rail.

For appearance it is best to counterbore the holes for the screws along the top of this support rail (and drill pilot holes for the screws in the top of the rear rail – see page 104).

Finally, screw the back support rail in place using zinc-plated Supascrews (see page 104) which won't rust, and plug the holes with wooden plugs or Brummer stopping.

13 Measure out and cut to length all the slats needed for the back of the bench and/or chair. Each of these then needs to be curved at the top and, again, I recommend a jigsaw for this job if you have one – if not, a coping saw. Once the basic curve has been achieved, use a

spokeshave to remove the saw cuts and then chamfer off *all* the edges of the slats – the sides as well as the tops. Alternatively an electric orbital sander will do this job very quickly. You should spend a lot of time on the slats for the back panel as this is the most prominent part of the finished bench.

If you wish, you can cut a decorative hole in the centre slat as I did. However, you really do need a jigsaw for this job. First draw the shape on the wood, drill a series of 3 pilot holes at one end, insert the blade of the jigsaw and cut along the pencil lines.

When all the slats are completed, screw them to the top back and back

support rails, again using zinc-plated Supascrews. At the top, the screw should pass from the back of the top back rail into the slats. (Make sure that they are the right length and don't break through the wood.) Counterbore these screws and plug the holes with dowelling or stopping. At the bottom, the screws pass from the front of the slats into the back support rail. Their heads are later hidden by the seat slats so they don't need to be counterbored but should be countersunk (see page 104).

An easy way to ensure you get the spacing of the slats right is to fix the centre panel in position first. Then cut a 'spacer' batten of waste wood to the

exact width of the spaces you want between the slats. By placing it between the fixed slat and the next one you are screwing in, you can help to increase both the accuracy and speed at which you work.

14 With all the slats in place you are ready to fit the seat itself. Cut all the battens required to length, noting that the foremost one is slightly wider than the rest.

Now chamfer off the edges of each one carefully – otherwise they will make sitting down for any length of time an uncomfortable experience! First run a jack plane along all the long edges and then smooth them off with a spokeshave or orbital sander. If you have an electric router, the 'rounding off' bit will do the whole job in one operation.

15 Now cut away the corners of the foremost slat using a tenon saw so that it will fit comfortably around the front legs. Having done that you are ready to screw all the slats in place. Do counterbore the screwholes and plug them afterwards otherwise the screw heads will show and spoil your handiwork.

16 The final construction stage is to cut out the arm rests and the twin tenons at the rear ends of these to fit into the mortice holes you cut on the face edge of the rear legs. If all your marking out was accurate the arm rests should be beautifully parallel!

Before glueing and screwing the arm rests in place, round off the corners and smooth the edges with a spokeshave or orbital sander. When the glue has cured in the twin mortice and tenon joint, screw the front of the arm to the top of the front leg, again taking care to counterbore the plug and holes neatly. (Ideally the screw should be 76mm (3in) long No. 10 and, of course, zinc-plated.)

17 The collapsible shelf is an optional but useful extra. If you decide to make it you will need to buy a length of brass piano hinge to attach it to the bench. (This is available from good ironmongers or specialist DIY shops but not normally at the DIY chain stores.) The advantage of this type of hinge is that it doesn't need to be recessed in the way that traditional hinges do.

Cut out the shelf, the lip that will help prevent things being knocked off it, and the 2 supports. Screw the lip along one side of the shelf and then screw a length of piano hinge along the underneath of the other side. Then screw the other flap of the hinge to the underneath of one of the arm rests.

Using a long stick to prop the shelf in the 'up' position, hold the shelf supports against the chair legs and pencil in where the piano hinge for these needs to go. Screw the hinge to the supports first and then to the inside edges of the front and rear legs. The supports need to fit tightly up against the underside of the shelf otherwise it will slope and so be highly unsafe for drinks!

18 Coat your finished bench and/or chair with a good wood preservative such as the Sadolin range (see page 107). Follow the maker's instructions carefully and if you are working in a garage or workshop make sure it's well ventilated. To ensure the bottoms of the legs get well impregnated, stand them all in a small container of the preservative for a day or so. Do remember that these products are poisonous and keep pets and children well away whilst you're treating the furniture.

Cutting list

Garden bench

Front leg	2 off	673 × 70 × 70mm (26½ × 2¾ × 2¾in)	Timber
Rear leg	2 off	1067 × 70 × 70mm (42 × 2¾ × 2¾in)	Timber
Arm rest	2 off	571 × 102 × 25mm (22½ × 4 × 1in)	Timber
Bottom rail	2 off	494 × 70 × 70mm (19½ × 2¾ × 2¾in)	Timber
Seat rail	2 off	494 × 89 × 32mm (19½ × 3½ × 1¼in)	Timber
Intermediate seat rails	2 off	521 × 89 × 32mm (20½ × 3½ × 1¼in)	Timber
Top back rail	1 off	1803 × 76 × 32mm (71 × 3 × 1¼in)	Timber
Front and rear rail	2 off	1803 × 152 × 32mm (71 × 6 × 1¼in)	Timber
Seat	3 off	1854 × 102 × 22mm (73 × 4 × ⅞in)	Timber
	1 off	1854 × 114 × 22mm (73 × 4½ × ⅞in)	Timber
Back support rail	1 off	1715 × 76 × 25mm (67½ × 3 × 1in)	Timber
Seat back	4 off	575 × 76 × 22mm (22⅝ × 3 × ⅞in)	Timber
	4 off	597 × 76 × 22mm (23½ × 3 × ⅞in)	Timber
	4 off	622 × 76 × 22mm (24½ × 3 × ⅞in)	Timber
	2 off	641 × 76 × 22mm (25¼ × 3 × ⅞in)	Timber
	2 off	660 × 76 × 22mm (26 × 3 × ⅞in)	Timber
	1 off	698 × 191 × 25mm (27½ × 7½ × 1in)	Timber
Shelf support	2 off	146 × 108 × 22mm (5¾ × 4¼ × ⅞in)	Timber
Shelf	1 off	394 × 223 × 25mm (15½ × 8¾ × 1in)	Timber
Shelf lip	1 off	394 × 51 × 9mm (15½ × 2 × ⅜in)	Timber

Ancillaries

	2 off	146mm (5¾in) brass piano hinge
	1 off	380mm (15in) brass piano hinge

Cutting list

Garden chair

Front leg	2 off	673 × 70 × 70mm (26½ × 2¾ × 2¾in)	Timber
Rear leg	2 off	1067 × 70 × 70mm (42 × 2¾ × 2¾in)	Timber
Arm rest	2 off	571 × 102 × 25mm (22½ × 4 × 1in)	Timber
Bottom rail	2 off	494 × 70 × 70mm (19½ × 2¾ × 2¾in)	Timber
Seat rail	2 off	494 × 89 × 32mm (19½ × 3½ × 1¼in)	Timber
Top back rail	1 off	533 × 76 × 32mm (21 × 3 × 1¼in)	Timber
Front and rear rail	2 off	533 × 152 × 32mm (21 × 6 × 1¼in)	Timber
Seat	3 off	584 × 102 × 22mm (23 × 4 × ⅞in)	Timber
	1 off	584 × 114 × 22mm (23 × 4½ × ⅞in)	Timber
Back support rail	1 off	445 × 76 × 25mm (17½ × 3 × 1in)	Timber
Seat back	2 off	641 × 76 × 22mm (25¼ × 3 × ⅞in)	Timber
	1 off	698 × 191 × 22mm (27½ × 7½ × ⅞in)	Timber
Shelf support	2 off	146 × 108 × 22mm (5¾ × 4¼ × ⅞in)	Timber
Shelf	1 off	394 × 223 × 25mm (15½ × 8¾ × 1in)	Timber
Shelf lip	1 off	394 × 51 × 9mm (15½ × 2 × ⅜in)	Timber

Ancillaries

	2 off	146mm (5¾in) brass piano hinge
	1 off	380mm (15in) brass piano hinge

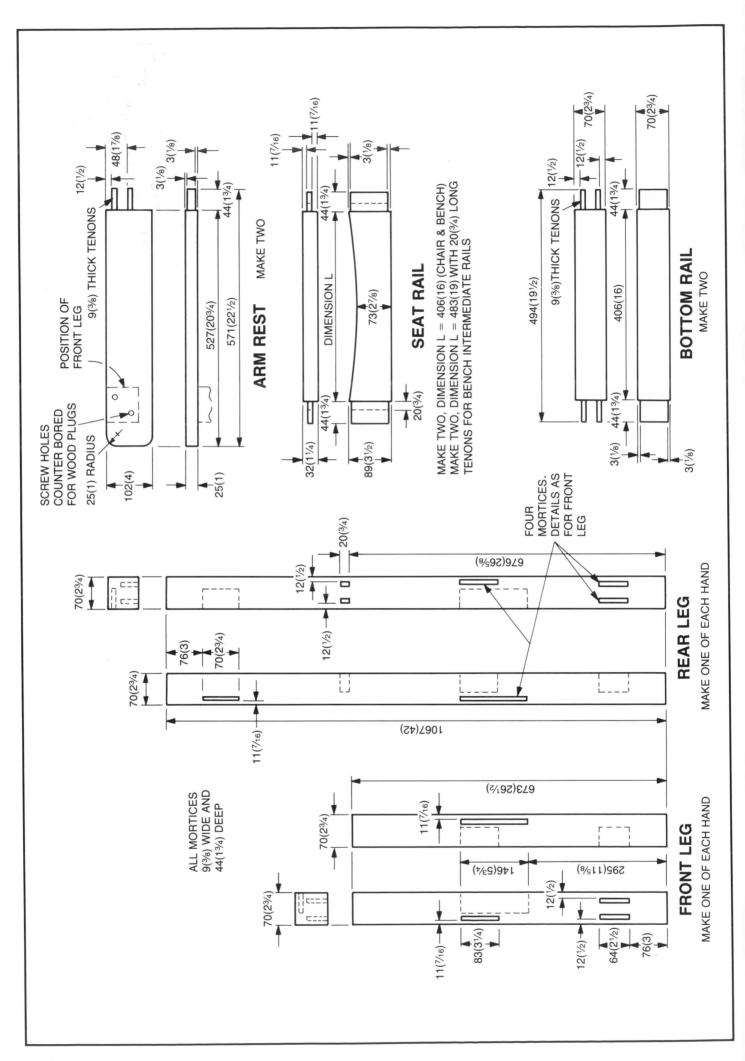

ARM REST MAKE TWO

48(1⅞)
12(½)
3(⅛) 3(⅛)
9(⅜) THICK TENONS
POSITION OF FRONT LEG
527(20¾)
44(1¾)
571(22½)
SCREW HOLES COUNTER BORED FOR WOOD PLUGS
25(1) RADIUS
102(4)
25(1)

SEAT RAIL

11(⁷⁄₁₆) 11(⁷⁄₁₆)
3(⅛)
44(1¾)
DIMENSION L
73(2⅞)
32(1¼)
44(1¾)
89(3½)
20(¾)

MAKE TWO, DIMENSION L = 406(16) (CHAIR & BENCH)
MAKE TWO, DIMENSION L = 483(19) WITH 20(¾) LONG
TENONS FOR BENCH INTERMEDIATE RAILS

BOTTOM RAIL MAKE TWO

70(2¾)
70(2¾)
12(½)
12(½)
44(1¾)
494(19½)
9(⅜)THICK TENONS
406(16)
44(1¾)
3(⅛)
3(⅛)

REAR LEG MAKE ONE OF EACH HAND

70(2¾)
20(¾)
12(½)
676(26⅝)
12(½)
76(3)
70(2¾)
70(2¾)
FOUR MORTICES. DETAILS AS FOR FRONT LEG
1067(42)
11(⁷⁄₁₆)

FRONT LEG MAKE ONE OF EACH HAND

ALL MORTICES 9(⅜) WIDE AND 44(1¾) DEEP
673(26½)
70(2¾)
11(⁷⁄₁₆)
146(5¾)
295(11⅝)
70(2¾)
12(½)
11(⁷⁄₁₆)
83(3¼)
12(½)
64(2½)
76(3)

80

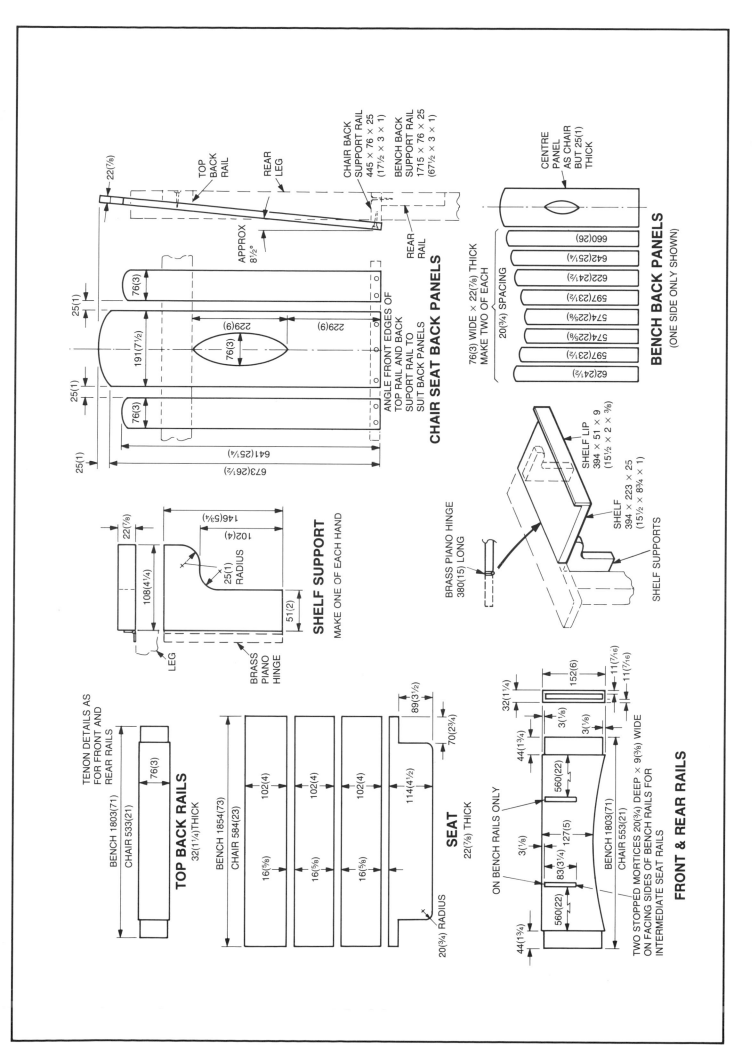

TOP BACK RAIL

REAR LEG

CHAIR BACK SUPPORT RAIL
445 × 76 × 25
(17½ × 3 × 1)

BENCH BACK SUPPORT RAIL
1715 × 76 × 25
(67½ × 3 × 1)

REAR RAIL

22(⅞)

APPROX 8½°

ANGLE FRONT EDGES OF TOP RAIL AND BACK SUPORT RAIL TO SUIT BACK PANELS

76(3)

25(1)

191(7½)

229(9)

76(3)

229(9)

25(1)

76(3)

25(1)

641(25¼)

673(26½)

CHAIR SEAT BACK PANELS

CENTRE PANEL AS CHAIR BUT 25(1) THICK

660(26)
642(25¼)
622(24½)
597(23½)
574(22⅝)
574(22⅝)
597(23½)
62(24½)

76(3) WIDE × 22(⅞) THICK MAKE TWO OF EACH

20(¾) SPACING

BENCH BACK PANELS
(ONE SIDE ONLY SHOWN)

22(⅞)

146(5¾)

102(4)

25(1) RADIUS

108(4¼)

51(2)

LEG

BRASS PIANO HINGE

SHELF SUPPORT

MAKE ONE OF EACH HAND

SHELF LIP
394 × 51 × 9
(15½ × 2 × ⅜)

SHELF
394 × 223 × 25
(15½ × 8¾ × 1)

SHELF SUPPORTS

BRASS PIANO HINGE
380(15) LONG

TENON DETAILS AS FOR FRONT AND REAR RAILS

76(3)

BENCH 1803(71)
CHAIR 533(21)

TOP BACK RAILS
32(1¼)THICK

BENCH 1854(73)
CHAIR 584(23)

102(4)

102(4)

102(4)

114(4½)

16(⅝)

16(⅝)

16(⅝)

89(3½)

70(2¾)

20(¾) RADIUS

SEAT
22(⅞) THICK

152(6)

11(⁷⁄₁₆)
11(⁷⁄₁₆)

32(1¼)

3(⅛)

3(⅛)

44(1¾)

560(22)

3(⅛)

127(5)

83(3¼)

560(22)

44(1¾)

BENCH 1803(71)
CHAIR 553(21)

ON BENCH RAILS ONLY

TWO STOPPED MORTICES 20(¾) DEEP × 9(⅜) WIDE ON FACING SIDES OF BENCH RAILS FOR INTERMEDIATE SEAT RAILS

FRONT & REAR RAILS

SUMMER HOUSE

Unfortunately many English summers turn out to be disappointing, so when the sun does shine, everybody wants to get out to make the most of it. If you have a sheltered area in your garden, you can enjoy sunshine nearly all the year round in a summer house that shields you from the cold wind, but lets you get the most from the warmth that floods in through the windows. The special feature of this summer house is that you can rotate it on its industrial castors. Rotate it to the east and catch the morning sun, which rapidly warms up the house just in time for a late breakfast (welcome in holiday times!). Rotate it throughout the day to follow the sun and when the evening comes, you can watch the sunset without the chill of the early evening. The ground for the summer house must be carefully prepared. The house can rotate equally well on carefully laid paving slabs, a patio or a specially prepared concrete base. Whichever option you choose, it is vital that it is flat.

Ventilation is provided for under the eaves of the roof, so that on very hot days air can circulate all the time without creating a draught. However, when winter winds blow, it is best to screw boards between the top of the walls and the roof to prevent any possibility of a storm lifting it off.

Don't be daunted by the size of the project or its complexity of construction – it really is not too difficult. The construction of the practically identical wall frames is mostly 'hammer-and-nails' carpentry. The base is straightforward, providing that you can use a protractor. The roof is a little more difficult, but I have devised a system of triangles for building it, so it is not as difficult as you might expect.

This is a really exciting project – something for all the family to enjoy – so sharpen your chisel, buy a new saw and have a go!

Materials

All woodworking jobs begin for me by selecting timber. For this particular job, I decided to buy 2 packs of 51 × 25mm (2 × 1in) timbers. This is a cheap way of buying your framing, but beware. Look it over carefully, because you must avoid timber with hundreds of knots. Spend a bit of time finding what you want and explain to the timber yard what you are making. I always find the merchants very helpful.

The floor is made from 2 sheets of shuttering grade plywood, the grade used for building construction. It has only one good face, which means it is less expensive, and as it is WPB grade (for outdoor use), it is excellent for this particular application. The timber used in between the sheets of ply is stock size. I bought sawn timber and then planed it all up but you may find it easier to buy planed all round timber (PAR).

Panelling in the roof frames is done with plywood (WPB grade once again) which is then covered with a medium-weight felt. The windows are crystal glaze plastic. On any rotating structure there will be certain stresses and strains, and this material is far more likely to stand up to them without cracking than glass.

The Floor

1   Start by marking out 30° angles onto the plywood to form the 6 sides. Use one of the existing sides as your first straight edge, and using a protractor mark off the 30° angle. You need 2 sheets to mark out each side. (There is quite a lot of waste – put it to one side to use for other projects.) The initial marking-out stage is critical. If you are not precise, you may end up with 6½ sides to your house!

2   Once you have pencilled in the 6 sides, use a panel saw (see page 98) to cut off the waste.

3   Lay the 2 pieces of plywood face down on a large flat surface (garage floor or drive will do) to form a hexagon and lay 3 timbers lengthways across the plywood (see plans). Using nails, spike the timbers to the plywood. ('Spiking' timber is a phrase used by carpenters when they fix nails through

the side of a piece of timber into another piece to prevent it moving.) This is a 'holding' operation aimed at keeping everything in place until the final nailing together.

4   Nail lengths of timber all around the edges, across the middle and across the outer edges. Stagger the timbers as you work and you will find it far easier to nail them in place. I use a medium-weight hammer and goggles for this sort of job just in case any splinters fly off. Cutting and fixing the timbers takes quite a while, but actually it is not vital to fix the timbers permanently at this stage. When you turn the whole hexagon over, you can drive nails through the plywood directly into the timbers below which is far easier.

5   Now cut out the 2 pieces of plywood for the second hexagon. Place them on the fixing timbers so that the centre join runs in the opposite direction to that of the first hexagon. This will add to the structural strength of the floor. (At this stage you will see just how accurate your marking out has been!)

Nail straight through the plywood into the framework below. Be generous with the nails and fix it well. Get someone to help you turn the hexagonal floor over so that nails can be driven through the plywood in exactly the same way.

6   Give the floor a very generous coating of wood preservative. On the underside particularly, I suggest 3 coats.

For instructions on how to fix the base so that it rotates, see page 86.

The Walls

If you look at any of the commercial garden sheds, you will find that the wall construction is usually a framework of wood onto which shiplap boards are nailed. These may be rather basic in design but they are very strong. Nevertheless a certain degree of accuracy is necessary when building them or the frame will not fit together.

1   Start by building yourself a framework to use as a kind of template. This way you will ensure that all the frames will be exactly the same. Perhaps

the simplest method is to buy an extra sheet of standard plywood which will be 1219mm (4 feet) wide and longer than needed for the walls. Screw battens of waste wood round the outer edges on 3 sides, and then mark out the length of the wall and fix another batten across at this point to give the height needed for the frame. This may seem a lengthy process for only 6 walls, but you will find it is well worth the effort.

2   Now cut all the battens needed for the frames for the 3 fully clad wall panels to length using the frame as your guide.

The sides of all the walls join each other at 30° angles so the outside edges of all the wall verticals must be cut to 30°. You can either pencil in the area to be removed and plane it off with a jack plane, or use an electric power plane (see page 105). Alternatively most big timber merchants have a bench circular saw which will do this job very quickly and efficiently for you if you prefer. (The greatest problem is not the actual planing of the 30° angle, but holding the narrow batten firmly while you work. You could buy wider timber, plane the 30° angle and then cut off the extra width, or another way around the problem would be to build each framework completely and then plane off the 30° angle. The drawback with this last method is that there is a danger of running into the nail heads that hold the frame together.)

3   Once the angles have been cut, assemble each framework with the 30° edges of the 2 verticals facing outwards. Nail the corners together first, using the following method. Using a G cramp, cramp the battens very firmly to the jig (plywood frame) and drill two small pilot holes for the nails to prevent the wood from splitting. You might need to experiment on a piece of waste wood first to get the correct hole size. The hole can be quite small. Nail all 4 corners together using large round wire nails. Nail a further vertical bar in the centre and 4 horizontal bars on either side, staggering them for extra rigidity.

4   Make the door frame in the same way, except that you need to double up the vertical battens to give strength for the doors. (You don't, of course, need a central or vertical battens for this frame.)

5   Make the frames for the window panels in the same way as for the other frames. The difference here is that the 4 horizontal bars are not 'staggered', but are level to form the window ledge. In addition you need to nail a further 4

short vertical battens between the horizontal ones.

6   Drill holes in the perspex panes for the windows and screw them in position. (Instructions for drilling and, if necessary, cutting this material are supplied by the manufacturer.)

Cladding
Now clad the frames with weatherproof boarding. Ready-machined boarding will be available from your timber merchant. There are a number of different styles, but all do the same basic job: they shed the rain from one board to the other without letting the wet into the house. The boarding is machined so that it interlocks.

1   First cut your cladding boards to width. At the bottom of the frames, I allowed a large overlap to get the water to drop off near the ground in the outside edge of the floor. This overlap forms a lip when you assemble the wall onto the base, and is a good location point.

2   Lay a framework flat on the garage floor or other flat surface. Fix the shiplap board in place using oval nails. (The oval shape helps prevent the nail from splitting the board.) When you reach the top of the framework with the last board, you may need to cut it to fit flush with the top of the frame. Clad the 3 wall panels fully from top to bottom and the 2 window walls only half way up.

The Doors
The two doors are constructed using mortice and tenon joints (see page 101). There are 3 horizontal bars in each door which are morticed and tenoned into the verticals.

1   Probably the most difficult part of making the doors is the correct marking out of these joints. The best way is to place the timber for the door frames, cut to length, in the framework and then pencil in the shoulder lines of the tenons on the horizontal door bars using the verticals as your measure.

2   Cut out all the joints following the instructions on page 101 and glue them together using waterproof glue such as Cascamite One Shot.

3   Now mortice out a slot in each door to take the mechanism for the door handle and catch. (Some woodworkers do this by drilling out most of the wood and then chiselling away the waste pieces. An electric drill in a bench stand works well for this, but there is always a

great deal of tidying up to do afterwards.)

4   Nail narrow battens of wood around the inside of the window area on each door to provide support for the perspex windows.

5   The window areas are designed to take panes of crystal glaze perspex exactly without the need to cut, but if you find you do have to cut it to fit, use a very fine-toothed saw. (Full instructions for cutting and drilling this material are usually provided with the packaging.)

To waterproof the windows I used mastic (available in several colours) and a mastic gun to apply it. Inject a bead all the way round the battens you glued to the frame and then press the perspex into position. Then inject another beading of mastic around the edge to seal the narrow gap between the perspex and the wood. This is a much simpler operation than using glass and putty.

6   Fit the shiplap board cladding in place on the lower half of each door.

Assembling the Walls
It is easier to assemble the floor and walls before the roof is made.

1   Set the base on its chosen site in the garden and get some helpers to stand the 3 fully clad walls and the window walls vertically in position. The 30° angles on the side walls should line up and the overlap boards on the bottoms of the walls should rest nicely against the base.

2   Drill pilot holes for the screws on the inside of the outer vertical battens. (An electric battery-driven screwdriver without a cable will make the job much easier.) Screw all the walls together using zinc-plated supascrews (see page 104) about 76mm (3in) long. Then pass screws through the bottom battens of the walls into the floor. When all the walls are secure, fit the door frame in place in the same way.

The Roof
At first, this may look a little difficult, but if you think of it as building a series of triangles, the task is not so daunting.

1   Start by drawing out the central triangular roof truss that goes right across the summer house full size on hardboard or on to the sheet of ply you used as a jig for building the side frames. It is far easier to mark the correct angles on the timbers when you have a full-size template to work to. Mark out, cut and nail together battens of timber to form triangular central roof trusses.

2   Again using the full-size drawing as a guide, make 4 more triangular trusses which are only *half* the length.

3   Place one of the full length triangular trusses across the middle of the roof. With someone to help, place 2 of the half roof trusses in position using the corners of the house as a guide. Pass screws through the centre upright of the full triangle into the uprights of the 2 half triangles. Now you have 3 trusses screwed together in the middle. Cut to length and screw on spacer battens between the triangles from the underside. When this half-roof section has been made, make the second half in the same way.

4   Take both sections down carefully and fit spacer battens between the triangles on the top side. This is more difficult as each cut needs to be at a 30° angle to get the battens to line up with the triangles. This is a fairly fiddly job and

I used an electric mitre saw to speed things up (see page 102).

5   Once both sections have been built, you will need to plane off some of the batten edges to allow the plywood 'skin' to lie flat on the framework, and also to treat the framework with wood preservative.

6   To 'skin' the roof you need 2 sheets of WPB plywood. Cut out the triangular sections as shown on the plan and nail them to the framework from underneath.

7   Use a medium density green felt to cover the plywood as a heavy felt is difficult to bend and fix. Use a marking knife with a new blade and a straight edge of wood or a long steel rule to cut the felt on a large offcut of plywood.

Nail the felt in position using galvanised felt nails with large heads. Double fold the bottom edge to provide a drip ledge. I started with a double fold on the bottom edge, tacked the felt in place, stretched it tight (a helpful 'assistant' is essential all through this job) and then fixed the top and sides. The nail heads look much better if you take the trouble to space them equally. Use a spare strip of timber with a heavy pencilled line to give you a guide as to where to drive them in. It's well worth the trouble.

8   Lift both felted sections back onto the top of the walls. Screw the 2 central trusses together along their length. Cut a small hexagonal plate out of plywood, position it under the centre of the 2 central trusses and pass screws through it into the bottom timbers.

Cut a strip of felt and fix it across the joint in the roof to waterproof the structure.

Making the house turn

The house turns by means of a single large raw bolt which is fitted through the centre of the floor and anchored into the paving slab or concrete base. Industrial castors make turning the house an easy job whatever your strength.

1   First buy the bolt and cut a piece of suitable waste plastic pipe to length to fit over it and form a 'sleeve'. Drill a hole through the floor the same diameter as the sleeve and fit the bolt and pipe in place. The bolt should not protrude more than, say, 6mm (¼in) above the floor or people may trip over it.

2   Screw an industrial castor underneath each of the 6 corners of the floor base. Instructions for fitting these are usually provided by the manufacturer.

3   Anchor the bottom of the bolt into a piece of metal piping set into concrete (as you would a rotating washing line).

4   Assemble the walls onto the base as explained above using bricks to prevent the house moving as you do so.

5   Secure the roof on top by passing screws through the battens at the top of the wall frames into the outer peripheral spacer battens of the roof structure.

6   Finally, hang the doors and fit the door handle and catch. I used self-recessing hinges for ease.

Fit a door stop by screwing a length of shiplap board, sawn in half vertically, to the outside of the door bearing the handle. Fit bolts on the inside face of the other door to hold it in position when closed.

Note: On a windy location make sure the wheels are 'chocked' when the house is not in use and that there are plenty of garden chairs loaded in it to weigh it down. Think of the embarrassing situation you could find yourself in on a windy March day chasing a 6-wheeled summer house down the road!

Cutting list

Floor	1 off	2438 × 70 × 44mm (96 × 2¾ × 1¾in)	Timber
	2 off	2064 × 70 × 44mm (81¼ × 2¾ × 1¾in)	Timber
	2 off	1670 × 70 × 44mm (65¾ × 2¾ × 1¾in)	Timber
	2 off	1270 × 70 × 44mm (50 × 2¾ × 1¾in)	Timber
Spacers	18 off	302* × 70 × 44mm (11⅞* × 2¾ × 1¾in)	Timber
End in-fills	12 off	375* × 70 × 44mm (14¾* × 2¾ × 1¾in)	Timber
Floor decking	4 off	2438 × 1219 × 12mm (96 × 48 × ½in)	WPB Exterior grade shuttering plywood
Roof: central roof truss	4 off	1441 × 44 × 25mm (56¾ × 1¾ × 1in)	Timber
	2 off	2438 × 44 × 25mm (96 × 1¾ × 1in)	Timber
Radial half roof truss	4 off	1403 × 44 × 25mm (55¼ × 1¾ × 1in)	Timber
	4 off	1181 × 44 × 25mm (46½ × 1¾ × 1in)	Timber
	6 off	303 × 44 × 25mm (11¹⁵⁄₁₆ × 1¾ × 1in)	Timber
Support plate	1 off	406 × 406 × 12mm (16 × 16 × ½in)	Plywood
Outer peripheral spacer battens	2 off	1353 × 44 × 25mm (53¼ × 1¾ × 1in)	Timber
	4 off	1337 × 44 × 25mm (52⅝ × 1¾ × 1in)	Timber
Inner spacer battens	2 off	711 × 38 × 25mm (28 × 1½ × 1in)	Timber
	4 off	695 × 38 × 25mm (27⅜ × 1½ × 1in)	Timber
Lower ties	2 off	813 × 44 × 25mm (32 × 1¾ × 1in)	Timber
	4 off	737 × 44 × 25mm (29 × 1¾ × 1in)	Timber
Cladding	2 off	2438 × 1219 × 5mm (96 × 48 × ³⁄₁₆in)	Plywood
Door frame	2 off	2029 × 41 × 25mm (79⅞ × 1⅝ × 1in)	Timber
	3 off	1137 × 44 × 25mm (44¾ × 1¾ × 1in)	Timber
	1 off	1187 × 44 × 25mm (46¾ × 1¾ × 1in)	Timber
	2 off	2029 × 25 × 25mm (79⅞ × 1 × 1in)	Timber
Doors	4 off	1886 × 70 × 25mm (74¼ × 2¾ × 1in)	Timber
	6 off	498 × 70 × 25mm (19⅝ × 2¾ × 1in)	Timber
	4 off	1084 × 20 × 12mm (42¾ × ¾ × ½in)	Timber
	4 off	422 × 20 × 12mm (16⅝ × ¾ × ½in)	Timber
Stop	1 off	762mm (30in) × 70mm (2¾in) wide shiplap board	
Cladding	14 off	562mm (22⅛in) shiplap board	
Windowed wall section (make 2)	2 off	2029 × 41 × 25mm (79⅞ × 1⅝ × 1in)	Timber
	2 off	1137 × 44 × 25mm (44¾ × 1¾ × 1in)	Timber
	1 off	1941 × 44 × 25mm (76⅜ × 1¾ × 1in)	Timber
	1 off	1337 × 44 × 25mm (52⅝ × 1¾ × 1in)	Timber
	4 off	547 × 44 × 25mm (21½ × 1¾ × 1in)	Timber
	4 off	280 × 44 × 25mm (11 × 1¾ × 1in)	Timber
	2 off	547 × 20 × 12mm (21½ × ¾ × ½in)	Timber
	2 off	1337mm (52⅝in) × 41mm (1⅝in) wide shiplap board	
Cladding	14 off	1219mm (48in) shiplap board	
Fully clad wall section (make 3)	2 off	2029 × 41 × 25mm (79⅞ × 1⅝ × 1in)	Timber
	2 off	1137 × 44 × 25mm (44¾ × 1¾ × 1in)	Timber
	1 off	1941 × 44 × 25mm (76⅜ × 1¾ × 1in)	Timber
	4 off	547 × 44 × 25mm (21½ × 1¾ × 1in)	Timber
Cladding	6 off	1219mm (48in) shiplap board	

*Will need minor length adjustments to suit actual assembly

Ancillaries

	6 off	76mm (3in) long self-recessing hinges
	1 off	Handle/latch assembly with latch plate
	2 off	127mm (5in) door bolts
	2 off	1124mm (44¼in) × 422mm (16⅝in) perspex for doors
	2 off	1293mm (50⅝in) × 1219mm (48in) perspex for windows
	1 off	15 metres (50ft) × 914mm (36in) roll of green medium-grade roofing felt
	2 off	Tubes plastic sealing compound
	6 off	Industrial castors
	1 off	Raw steel bolt
	1 off	Plastic piping (waste) to cover bolt

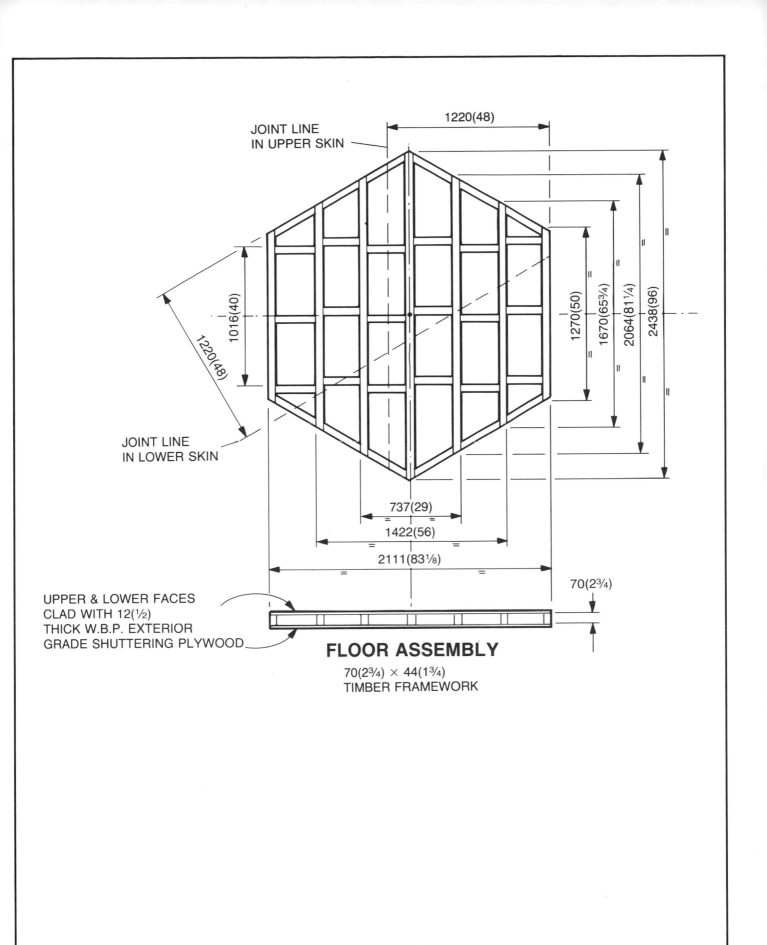

JOINT LINE
IN UPPER SKIN

1220(48)

JOINT LINE
IN LOWER SKIN

1016(40)

1220(48)

1270(50)

1670(65¾)

2064(81¼)

2438(96)

737(29)

1422(56)

2111(83⅛)

70(2¾)

UPPER & LOWER FACES
CLAD WITH 12(½)
THICK W.B.P. EXTERIOR
GRADE SHUTTERING PLYWOOD

FLOOR ASSEMBLY

70(2¾) × 44(1¾)
TIMBER FRAMEWORK

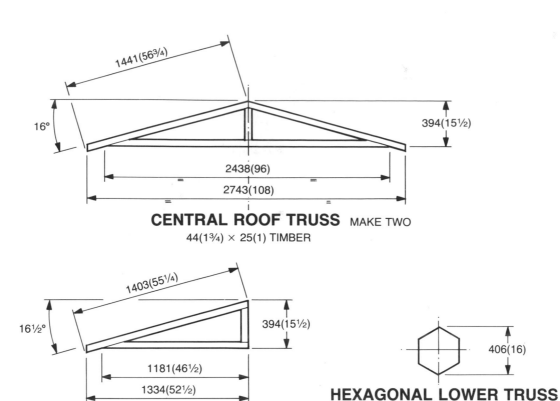

CENTRAL ROOF TRUSS MAKE TWO
44(1¾) × 25(1) TIMBER

1441(56¾)

16°

394(15½)

2438(96)

2743(108)

1403(55¼)

16½°

394(15½)

1181(46½)

1334(52½)

RADIAL HALF ROOF TRUSS
MAKE FOUR
44(1¾) × 25(1) TIMBER

406(16)

HEXAGONAL LOWER TRUSS
SUPPORT PLATE
12(½) WB PLYWOOD

CENTRAL ROOF
TRUSS

RADIAL HALF
ROOF TRUSS'S

A

OUTER
SPACER

INTER
SPACER

LOWER
TIE

14(⁹⁄₁₆)

SUPPORT
PLATE

SUPPORT
PLATE

LOWER TIE

INTER SPACER

VIEW ON ARROW 'A'
ILLUSTRATING ARRANGEMENT
OF INTER SPACER, LOWER TIE & SUPPORT PLATE

ROOF ASSEMBLY
TOP SURFACES CLAD WITH 5(³⁄₁₆)
THICK WPB PLYWOOD AND COVERED
WITH GREEN MEDIUM GRADE
ROOFING FELT

Garden bench and chair

Summer house

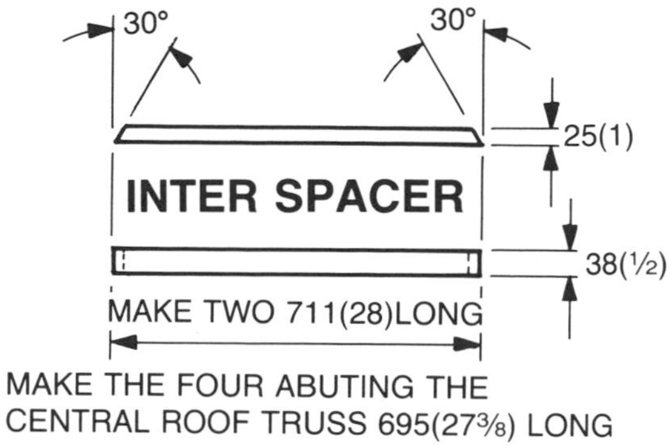
30°
30°
25(1)
INTER SPACER
38(½)
MAKE TWO 711(28)LONG
MAKE THE FOUR ABUTING THE
CENTRAL ROOF TRUSS 695(27⅜) LONG

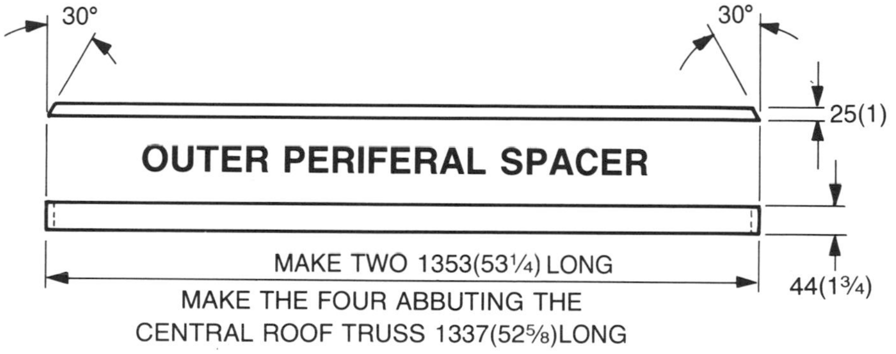
30°
30°
25(1)
OUTER PERIFERAL SPACER
MAKE TWO 1353(53¼) LONG
44(1¾)
MAKE THE FOUR ABBUTING THE
CENTRAL ROOF TRUSS 1337(52⅝)LONG

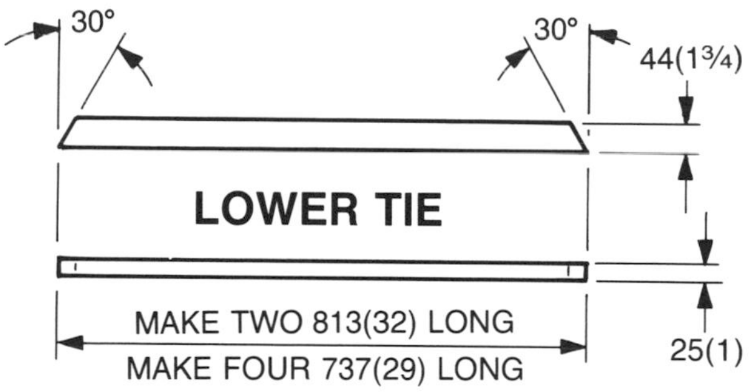
30°
30°
44(1¾)
LOWER TIE
MAKE TWO 813(32) LONG
MAKE FOUR 737(29) LONG
25(1)

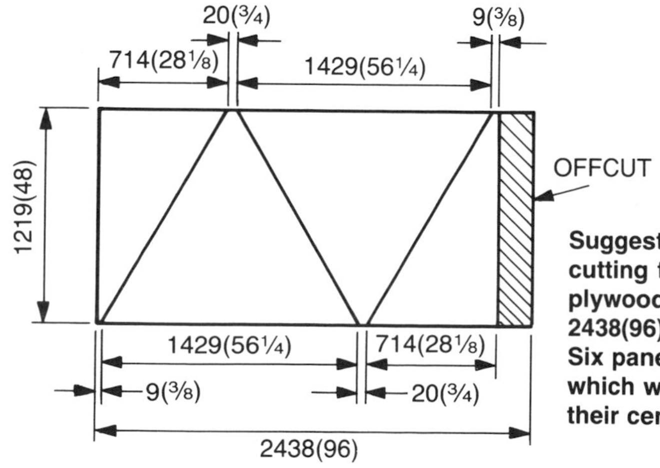
20(¾)
9(⅜)
714(28⅛)
1429(56¼)
1219(48)
OFFCUT
1429(56¼)
714(28⅛)
9(⅜)
20(¾)
2438(96)

Suggested method for cutting the 5(3/16) thick plywood panels from two 2438(96) × 1219(48) sheets. Six panels required, two of which will have a joint along their centre line

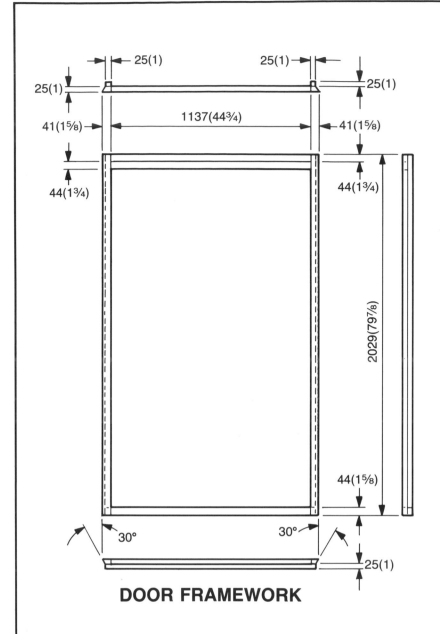

DOOR FRAMEWORK

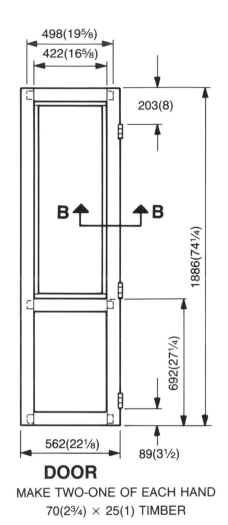

DOOR

MAKE TWO-ONE OF EACH HAND
70(2¾) × 25(1) TIMBER

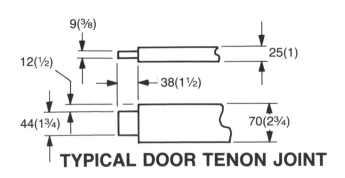

TYPICAL DOOR TENON JOINT

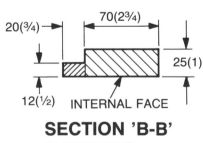

SECTION 'B-B'

ILLUSTRATING
'WINDOW' BEADING

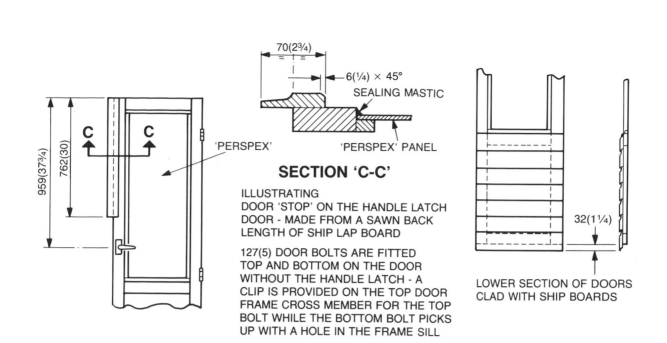

SECTION 'C-C'

ILLUSTRATING
DOOR 'STOP' ON THE HANDLE LATCH
DOOR - MADE FROM A SAWN BACK
LENGTH OF SHIP LAP BOARD

127(5) DOOR BOLTS ARE FITTED
TOP AND BOTTOM ON THE DOOR
WITHOUT THE HANDLE LATCH - A
CLIP IS PROVIDED ON THE TOP DOOR
FRAME CROSS MEMBER FOR THE TOP
BOLT WHILE THE BOTTOM BOLT PICKS
UP WITH A HOLE IN THE FRAME SILL

LOWER SECTION OF DOORS
CLAD WITH SHIP BOARDS

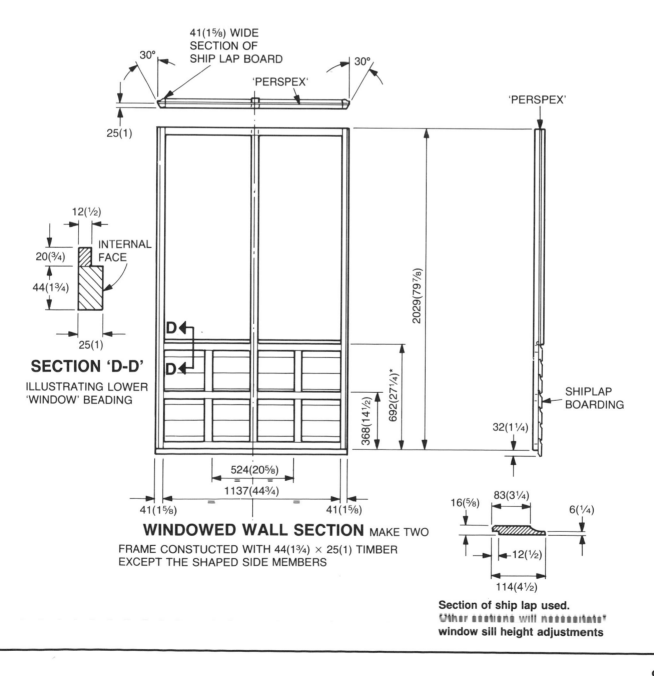

SECTION 'D-D'

ILLUSTRATING LOWER
'WINDOW' BEADING

WINDOWED WALL SECTION MAKE TWO

FRAME CONSTUCTED WITH 44(1¾) × 25(1) TIMBER
EXCEPT THE SHAPED SIDE MEMBERS

Section of ship lap used.
Other sections will necessitate'
window sill height adjustments

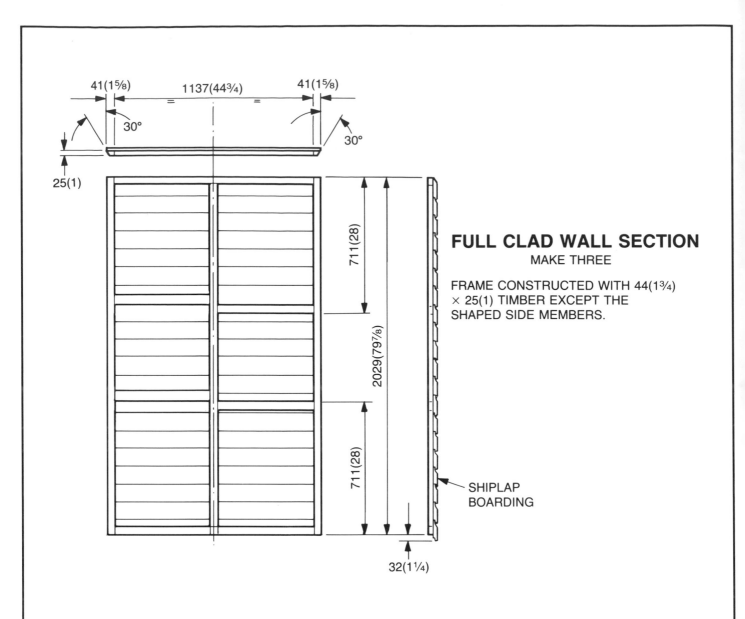

41(1⅝) 1137(44¾) 41(1⅝)

30° 30°

25(1)

711(28)

2029(79⅞)

711(28)

32(1¼)

FULL CLAD WALL SECTION
MAKE THREE

FRAME CONSTRUCTED WITH 44(1¾)
× 25(1) TIMBER EXCEPT THE
SHAPED SIDE MEMBERS.

SHIPLAP
BOARDING

FOLLOWING THE PLANS

Depending on the complexity of each part to be made, the plan sheets show one, two or three views - usually top, front and side.

Various types of lines and symbols are used in these views to indicate different features. The example on this page will help you understand what they mean.

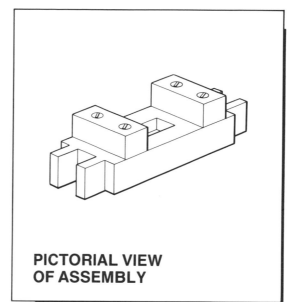

PICTORIAL VIEW OF ASSEMBLY

DIMENSIONED PLAN VIEWS OF ASSEMBLY

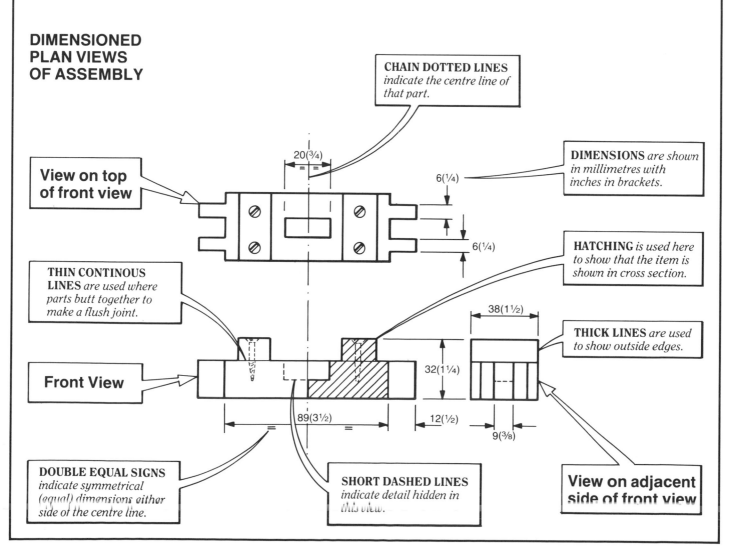

CHAIN DOTTED LINES indicate the centre line of that part.

View on top of front view

DIMENSIONS are shown in millimetres with inches in brackets.

20(¾)

6(¼)

6(¼)

THIN CONTINOUS LINES are used where parts butt together to make a flush joint.

HATCHING is used here to show that the item is shown in cross section.

38(1½)

THICK LINES are used to show outside edges.

32(1¼)

Front View

89(3½)

12(½)

9(⅜)

DOUBLE EQUAL SIGNS indicate symmetrical (equal) dimensions either side of the centre line.

SHORT DASHED LINES indicate detail hidden in this view.

View on adjacent side of front view

TOOLS AND TECHNIQUES

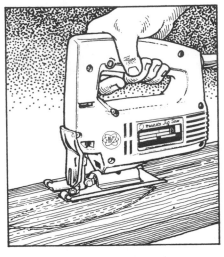

Cutting timber

However carefully you buy your timber or even design your projects around stock sizes, at some stage it is always necessary to do a certain amount of cutting.

Converting timber to useful lengths and widths was traditionally a job for the panel saw. The best of these saws have wooden handles and taper ground backs and are beautiful to hold and use. A recent development in the design of this saw was the introduction of hard point teeth, largely in response to the problems of cutting the tough man-made boards available nowadays. These teeth stay sharper for much longer, but when they do blunt off it's impossible to sharpen them in the traditional way.

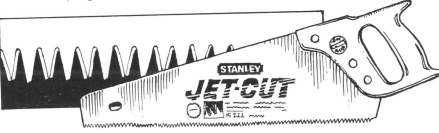

The latest development of the panel saw by Stanley Tools is the introduction of the 'Jet-Cut' model. The teeth on these saws are unique in that they allow the tool to cut on both the forward and reverse strokes making sawing operations very quick. All Jet-Cut saws have hardened teeth.

The tenon saw (illustrated on opposite page) is absolutely indispensable for all accurate cutting. The cheaper ones have a steel back, while the more expensive have a heavier brass back which makes the cutting process even easier. Tenon saws are also available with hardened teeth.

The electric-powered hand saw is a really speedy and accurate tool for cutting both timber and man-made boards. However, one of the dangers with this tool is the tendency for the teeth to 'blunt off' very

rapidly. The saw may then raise itself and skate across the timber. Therefore I would advise you to choose one fitted with a tungsten carbide blade which will stay sharp for a long time and when it does blunt will do so gradually. It can then be sharpened by the supplier.

To my mind there is one tool that has changed woodworking more dramatically than any other in recent years – the electric router. Not only will it cut shaping and mouldings, but also a variety of traditional joints, such as rebates (illustrated above), housing joints and even dovetails.

The router cuts wood at very high speed so look for safety features such as an on-off switch actually in the handle, and a perspex shield to prevent the chips accidentally flying out into the operator's face. A 3-turret head adjustment for depth of cut is also very helpful.

The most commonly bought electric cutting tool is usually the jigsaw. There are many variations of this tool around, but an absolute must when selecting one is to make sure that the tool you buy has a small roller guide wheel fitted at the back of the blade. It is also useful to have a tool with a speed control. When cutting man-made boards you'll need to experiment with both the best speed to use and the rate of feed (how fast you push it) to get the neatest result.

Jigsaws are excellent for cutting large curved shapes in plywood. They are also able to cut internal holes such as that featured on the back of the garden bench (see page 91). The jigsaw's main limitation is that it can't work in very thick wood as the blade has a tendency to bend at the bottom.

One of the most pleasing hand tools to use is the plane. There are a great number of these in all shapes and sizes, but it's the jack plane that is probably my favourite. It is larger than a smoothing plane and so is very useful in everyday work – that's why it became called 'Jack of all trades'. Its other advantage is the sole length and the distance between the mouth of the plane and the front. This distance is important particularly if you are working on end grain held in a vice. I used a jack plane to remove the waste wood from around the raised field on the pine blanket chest (see page 45), after initially ploughing a groove with a plough plane. In my workshop it's the tool that falls to hand for the majority of my planing jobs and also for cutting chamfers.

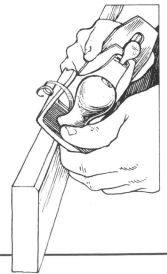

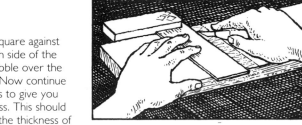

Housing joint

The housing joint is a good basic joint to learn and is very strong. It is most commonly used in shelving.

Onto the piece of timber that is to be cut away, mark the width of the timber to be slotted in. An easy way to do this is to mark round the timber itself, making sure it is at 90° by holding a carpenter's square against one side of it. Mark along each side of the timber with a pencil, then scribble over the waste wood to be removed. Now continue the pencil lines down the sides to give you the depth of the housing recess. This should not be more than two thirds the thickness of the wood.

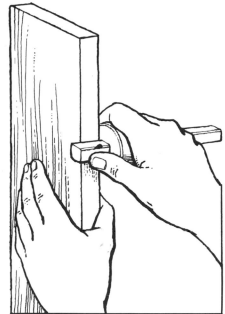

Go over the pencil lines with a marking knife and use a marking gauge to scribe the depth of the housing on the sides of the timber so that the wood fibres on the surface are cut and when sawing starts you won't get jagged edges. Fix the wood firmly to the bench and, with a sharp tenon saw, cut carefully down the lines to the full depth of the housing.

Using a firmer or bevel-edged chisel and a mallet, chop out the waste wood working from both sides of the wood into the middle. The awkward part is getting the bottom of the recess completely flat so that the joint will clamp up squarely. This can be done with a chisel, but you will need to use a steel rule to keep checking the depth. The more traditional way is to use a hand router which will ensure that the recess is of a uniform depth. Today the electric router (*bottom right*) has taken over not only the chisel's job of removing the wood, but also the task of seeing that the housing is of a uniform depth all along its length. However, there is still a great sense of achievement and satisfaction in cutting these joints by hand.

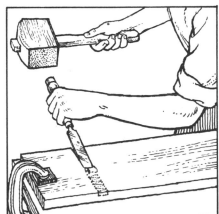

Stopped housing joint

A stopped housing joint (*bottom left*) is one where the housing, or recess, is not cut right along the timber but stops before the end in order to conceal it from view. When marking out the recess, measure back from the face edge a small distance. This will form the 'stop' and must not be cut out. Use a chisel and mallet to chip out a small square behind the stop, then chop the square to the full depth required. Insert the tip of the tenon saw into the square and work backwards along the marking knife lines. Then continue as for a normal housing.

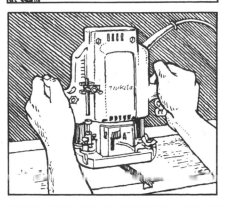

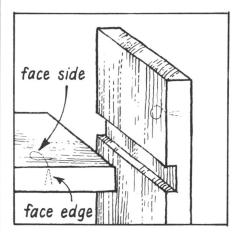

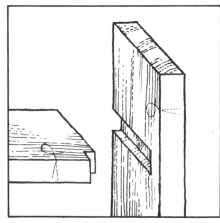

face side

face edge

Face side and face edge

Always mark the side and edge of a piece of timber that you want to be most visible at an early stage of a project. You can then refer to these marks when cutting any joints, grooves and chamfers.

Halving joint

A halving joint is so called because you cut away half the wood from each of the 2 pieces to be joined. It is an extremely useful basic joint.

Use a carpenter's square and pencil, and then a marking knife to mark the width of

the area to be cut away. Then use a marking gauge to mark the depth of the joint. If the joint is at the end of a piece of wood you can cut away the waste using a tenon saw. If not, you will need to use a tenon saw to cut down to the correct depth and a chisel to pare out the waste.

Mortice and tenon joints

The mortice and tenon joint is one of the most versatile and useful methods of jointing pieces of wood together. The mortice is the hole or slot and the tenon is the peg that fits into it. Over the years woodworkers have produced many variations of this joint which are not just the quirks of individuals, but have practical purposes. The basic joint is a *through* mortice and tenon where the mortice hole is cut right through the timber and the end of the tenon peg can be seen. This type of joint is sometimes assembled using wedges of wood to increase the rigidity of the peg in the mortice. It has only been used on the screen in this book (see page 13). Elsewhere I have used the stopped mortice and tenon and variations of this.

Stopped stub mortice and tenon

The diagram *below* shows the marking out you need to master before any cutting starts. Begin by marking what are called the 'shoulder' lines of the tenon. Measure the

depth of the tenon peg you need onto the wood and use a pencil and carpenter's square to draw the shoulder line across the side of the timber, and then right round the rail. (If you have to make several identical joints you can save time and increase your accuracy by clamping the rails together and drawing the shoulder lines on 2 sides of the timber in 1 operation. Then unclamp the pieces and continue the lines right round.) Select a firmer or mortice chisel that is approximately a third the width of the tenon rail. (This does not have to be exact – it's just a rule of thumb.) Set the points of your mortice gauge so that the chisel just fits between them. A mortice gauge has 2 marking points, 1 of which is adjustable to allow for different widths of chisel. It also has a sliding fence so that the 2 gauge points can scribe the same width on any depth of timber. A central screw or locking device holds both the adjustable point and the fence firmly in position once the gauge has been set up. Setting the gauge fence so as to get the 2 points in the centre of the tenon rail is done

by trial and error. Hold the fence against one side of the rail and press the 2 points into the wood. Then turn the gauge round and place it on the other side of the rail. If both points line up with the holes, the fence is in the right place, but if not keep adjusting it and repeating the procedure until they do. Once the gauge has been set, don't alter it as it is needed for marking out both tenon and mortice.

Now mark in the width of the tenon peg by dragging the gauge points from 1 shoulder line up and over the end of the rail to the opposite shoulder line.

Use the tenon rail itself to mark the length of the mortice hole in pencil. (Again, if you are making more than 1 identical joint clamp the timbers together and mark them all at the same time.) Scribe in the width of the mortice using your mortice gauge. Then reduce the length of the hole by a small amount – about 3mm (⅛in) – at each end. This is so that if the tenon rail shrinks the hole will remain hidden. An appropriate adjustment is also made when making the tenon peg (see *opposite*).

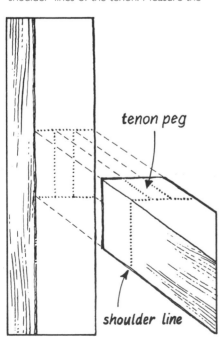

tenon peg

shoulder line

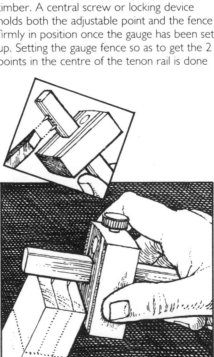

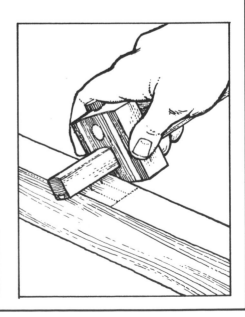

Chopping out the mortice hole is best done over the sturdiest place on the workbench. This is normally at one end of the bench over the leg. Fit the timber to be chopped to the bench using a 'G' clamp. Don't be tempted to fit the wood in a vice for 2 reasons: 1) constant heavy chopping of mortices in a vice weakens the bolt mounting holes; 2) as the underside of the piece of timber is not supported the chisel may break the wood out at the back. Don't hurry the chiselling – take a light row of chippings out at a time. Use the wedge-shaped blade of the mortice chisel so that as the blade edge enters the wood it raises the chip up. Use a pencil line or piece of tape on the back of the chisel to help you gauge when the

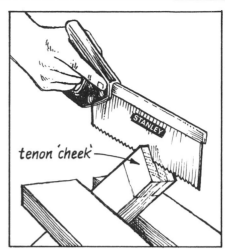

correct depth of the mortice has been reached. Try not to lever out the chips by letting the chisel shank press on the end of the mortice hole, otherwise you will have a 'bruised' hole and it will always show.

Scribe in all the pencil lines on the tenon rail with a marking knife before you start cutting. The marking knife cuts through all the surface wood fibres so that when you cut off the tenon 'cheeks' you will be left with clean edges. A tenon saw is essential for cutting the tenon as it has a steel or brass stiffener along its back which keeps it rigid and gives you plenty of control.

    Fix your tenon rail in the vice at about 45°. Cut down one side of the tenon peg as far as the shoulder line, but only half way along the top edge. Reverse the wood in the vice and repeat exactly the same operation. Now fix the wood at 90° to the bench top and complete the cut, taking it all the way down to the shoulder line. What you are aiming to do in the first 2 cuts is to provide the saw blade with 'guide slots' for the final cut. This may sound rather a long method of achieving a tenon, but it is accurate and works well. Repeat for the other side of the peg. Finally, fix the rail to the bench using a bench block and cut across the shoulder lines to remove the 'cheeks'.

    Ideally you should now reduce the depth of the tenon peg on either side by the same amount as you reduced the size of the mortice hole (see *opposite*), so that the joint will remain hidden even if the wood shrinks.

tenon 'cheek'

Twin mortice and tenons

Where really thick pieces of timber are being jointed as with the garden bench and chair (page 69), then a twin mortice and tenon should be used. This is because to chisel out a huge mortice hole for 1 thick tenon would weaken the wood, so you cut 2 mortice holes and a pair of tenons to fit. The marking out procedure and cutting out are the same. The only extra task is the removal of the waste timber between the 2 tenons. Do this by cutting down to the shoulder lines in the same way as for the tenon cheeks and use a coping saw to cut across the bottom and a chisel to finish off.

Haunched mortice and tenons

A haunched mortice and tenon joint is called for whenever a wide rail has to be fixed into an upright. If the mortice hole were chopped out to the full depth of the rail, the upright would be weakened by the removal of so much timber. If a narrower tenon were used, the rail would not be fixed securely and would be prone to twist, so the solution is to cut away part of the tenon.

    These joints are used on both tables (page 57) and the blanket chest (page 45).

    However, they have a different type of haunch for each project. The joints for the table legs have square

haunches and those for the blanket chest corner posts have bevelled ones.

With the table a square haunch (*below left*) is acceptable as the top of the table hides the joint from view. Cut the tenon peg in the normal way, then mark out and remove the waste piece to form the haunch using a tenon saw. When you come to chop out the mortice remember that you are cutting to 2 different depths. The final procedure when making these joints for the table is to cut a 45° bevel on the end of the tenon peg so that it fits against the tenon peg of the rail coming into the leg at right angles to it.

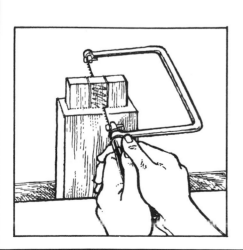

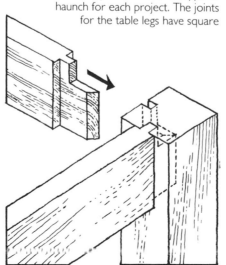

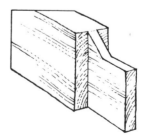

With the corner posts of the blanket chest the haunches have to be bevelled (see *above*) so that the joints can't be seen when the lid is lifted. Cut a square haunch first, then draw a diagonal line across from the top of the rail to the opposite corner of the haunch and cut away the triangular waste piece.

Cutting grooves

There are many jobs in woodworking that require grooves to be cut and the traditional tool for this is the plough plane (see *below*). These very versatile tools come complete with a set of cutters of different widths for different jobs.

First adjust the cutter you have selected so that it takes off a fine shaving. Then adjust the fence so that, with this against the edge of the wood, the cutter is positioned where you need the groove. Finally, set the depth stop. Start at the front of the piece of timber and move steadily towards the back, removing shavings as you go. (I have always found it an advantage to rub candle wax on the soles of plough planes to help them work more smoothly.) Don't force the tool – if you have set it up correctly it will stop removing shavings when the correct depth is reached. You can also use an electric router for cutting grooves (see page 98).

Raised fielded panels

Cutting raised fielded panels as for a blanket chest (page 45) is another job where the plough plane is of great use. After marking out the shape of your raised panel, this tool can be used to remove the waste around the fielded section.

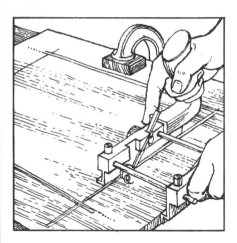

First fix the panel firmly to the bench which I find is best achieved by using 2 'G' clamps. If you work over the corner of the work bench you will be able to fix both clamps and still allow room for the plane to work. First cut a groove along the *waste side* of your pencil line *with* the grain. Do the same on the opposite side. Now you have to cut *across* the grain. With a marking knife, go over the pencil lines for these 2 sides cutting deeply into the grain. Now you can plough along the waste side of these lines. Sometimes it is necessary to stop ploughing and repeat the operation with the marking knife. If you don't cut very cleanly through the wood fibres with a knife first the cutter will tear the grain out and the panel will be spoilt.

Once the initial groove has been cut around the 'field' use a jack or smoothing plane (see pages 98 and 105) to remove the rest of the waste. I always leave panels like this just a little bigger and thicker than

required until I get to the panel-fitting stage when I can make the final adjustments accurately.

Mitring

In most woodworking projects I find that a butt joint never looks as nice as a mitre. The top of the black ash table (page 59) is a typical example. The mitre joints at the corners look far more 'finished' than the butt joints on the benches. However, more skill is needed to cut mitres, especially large ones as are needed for the table top.

The first essential tool for this job is a sliding bevel gauge. Set the gauge to 45° and, working from the face side, face edge (see page 99), pencil in the mitre line on each piece of wood. Go over the pencil lines with a marking knife. Place the wood in a mitre block and line up your marked line with the appropriate slots. Then use a tenon saw to cut the timber. The best mitre blocks have little brass 'lugs' at the top to prevent the saw blade wearing away the sides. (You will probably find that all the commercially available mitre blocks are too small to take the table surrounds, in which case clamp the timber firmly to your workbench, ensure your tenon saw is really sharp and follow the 'knifed-in' line accurately. Be careful to keep the saw at 90° to the wood.)

Probably the most rapid and accurate way of cutting mitres nowadays is to use an electric mitre saw. I used one of these for some of the timbers in the summer house (page 83). The saw cuts down onto a bed and the sawing assembly is fitted to a 'protractor' which swivels to give the various angles. These are excellent machines but you might need to make a few dozen picture frames to cover its initial cost!

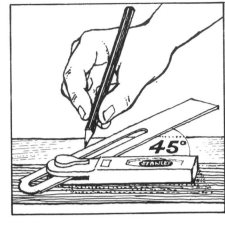

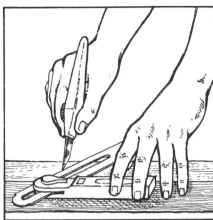

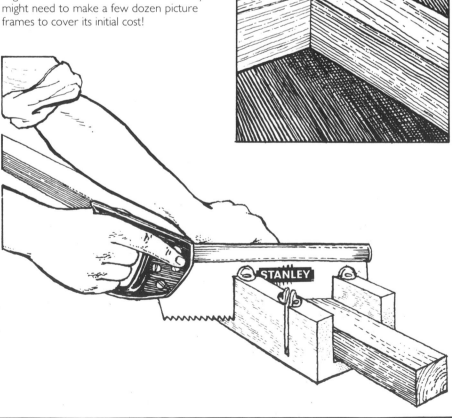

Joining planks

When making furniture it is frequently necessary to join planks together to get the width you require. Even if you spend out on top-quality timber you will probably still find it best to join planks as the wider the plank, the more unstable it becomes. Ideally select planks 51–102mm (2–4in) wide and before you join them look at the direction of the growth rings on the ends and arrange them so that they run in opposite directions (see *below*). This way if a plank moves, the movement will be counteracted by the other planks.

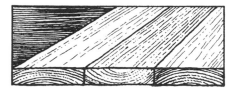

Rub joint

The most simple method of fixing planks together is rub jointing. Make sure that the edges to be joined are flat and square and if not use the jointer plane as described under *Dowel joint*. Once this is done, score the edges to create a larger glueing area. Fix a plank in the vice, apply glue to one edge, put another plank on top, and then rub the 2 planks together from side to side to make sure the glue works into the wood fibres. Then sash cramp the planks together. Modern glues are often stronger than the wood fibres themselves, so if you make a good rub joint you should have no difficulties.

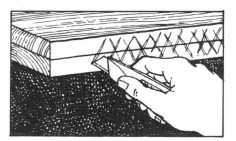

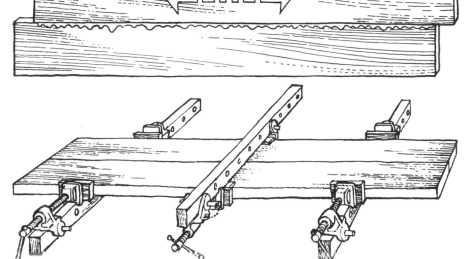

Dowel joint

Major improvements in glues have made many jointing methods obsolete, but nevertheless it is sometimes advisable to join planks with dowels as well as glue (as with the table and bench tops on page 58).

Select the face sides of your planks (very important with a table top) and arrange the end grain. Then place all the timbers on their sides and clamp them together. Using a carpenter's square, mark the positions for the dowel rods across the edges of the planks. Separate all the planks and, using a marking gauge, mark the centres for the dowel rod holes.

Drill the holes for the dowels making sure that they are at 90° in both planes. This is easy if you have a drill stand, but if not use a carpenter's square as a guide and take your time.

When you come to fit the planks together you may need to plane or 'shoot' the edges using a jointer plane. These are the longest planes made and are expensive to buy, but you can hire them. Check the plank edges first by standing one on top of the other, and if you can see daylight through any of them then you need to use this plane.

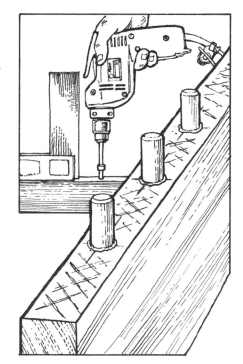

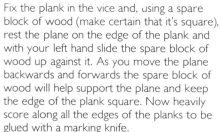

Fix the plank in the vice and, using a spare block of wood (make certain that it's square), rest the plane on the edge of the plank and with your left hand slide the spare block of wood up against it. As you move the plane backwards and forwards the spare block of wood will help support the plane and keep the edge of the plank square. Now heavily score along all the edges of the planks to be glued with a marking knife.

Fluted wooden dowel rods are now available with bevelled ends which are ideal for this joint. Otherwise cut ordinary dowel rod into lengths and chamfer off the ends. Apply glue to the ends of the dowel rods and tap them firmly into the holes using a hammer and a block of waste wood. Then apply glue to the scored edges of the planks and to the other ends of the dowels. Fit all the planks together and use sash cramps to hold them in position while the glue 'cures' (dries). Arrange the cramps with some below and some on top (these can be hired).

Drilling and screwing

Besides glue and joints to hold timber together there are, of course, a great number of different types of screw. In some areas of carpentry nails are the most efficient means of holding timber together, e.g. roof joists, and often the nail and hammer are the novice's first introduction to woodworking. However, when you use screws there are some further techniques that must be learned. Firstly never use a hammer to put a screw into a plank. Nails will draw out so pieces of wood fixed together with nails can be prised apart. But the thread of a screw grips the wood and can only be removed if properly driven in using a screwdriver. What's more, screws should never be driven straight into wood without a pilot hole being drilled first, otherwise you may find it becomes completely immobile half way in or, worse, the head shears off. Drill a hole using a bit the diameter of the piece of steel in the centre of the screw. Then, as the screw is driven into the wood, it is only the threads that will pull into the wood fibres and you should be able to insert and, if necessary, remove it easily.

Many screwing jobs also require a countersink. This useful little tool bores out a hole just big enough for the screw head to fit in so allowing it to lie flush with the surface.

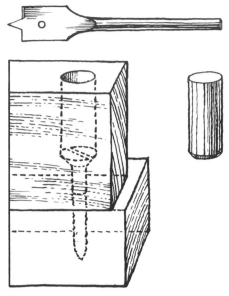

Sometimes when you have 2 particularly deep pieces of timber to screw together it's not practical to buy massive screws. Instead you can drill large holes to take the complete screw well below the surface. This is called counterboring (see *above*). Ideally the drill bit used should be just a little larger than the head of the screw. The holes can then be disguised with plugs of dowel rod.

Screws have changed quite a lot in the last few years. The traditional screw with the single slot for the screwdriver blade is being rapidly superseded by the new cross head or Supascrew. Supascrews are a real advance as the drive is much more positive than with the old type. It's not just the head that is different, it's also that the twin threads on the Supascrew speed up the driving in process. The new threads are also a better shape for getting a good hold in man-made boards. You will also find that after a number of years in place the screw is easier to retract than the old ones.

The very latest type of screw available is called a 'Multi'. It has a completely new head which takes a special screwdriver bit so that there is almost no chance of it slipping. What's more, the eye doesn't notice this small square hole as much as a slot or cross. The other advantage of this new screw is that it is coloured. This means that you can buy the colour that matches your timber as I did for the teak-faced blanket chest (page 19). Multis are available in a full range of sizes and are manufactured by European Industrial Services Ltd (see page 108).

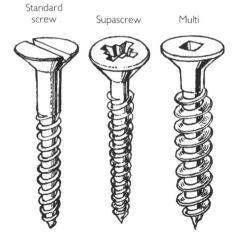

Standard screw   Supascrew   Multi

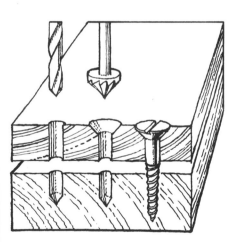

The battery-powered screwdriver (*above right*) has become very popular in the last 5 years – what ever did we do before they were invented? Some makes have refinements such as clutches with different torque settings which are very useful. Most have a switch for selecting forward or reverse, and some even have a progressive trigger action, which is a great help when starting off screws. A battery charger is provided with the tool and the whole unit is very compact allowing DIY-ers to do jobs around the home and garden without being encumbered by a long tangle of electric cable.

The traditional hand drill (*right*) still finds a place in my tool box. I mostly use it for drilling very fine holes. With a hand drill you can feel very accurately just how the drilling of a hole is going.

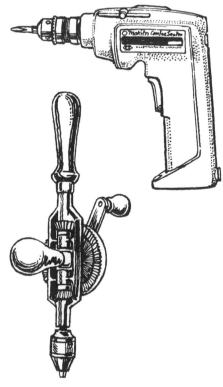

Not only have screws improved over the last few years, but also the drivers (*below*). A good quality screwdriver will last for many years (providing, that is, that you don't use it for opening cans!).

Perhaps the most efficient hand-powered screwdriver is the Yankee. These screwdrivers have both a ratchet action and a pump action. The shaft of the screwdriver is milled and when pressure is applied to the handle it turns the screwdriver blade. Not only are these screwdrivers fast in action, but they are also very versatile as you can buy a range of drill and countersink bits for them.

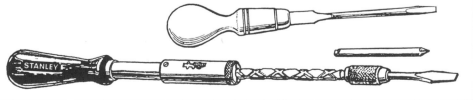

Planing and finishing timber

The initial preparation of timber is very important. As I have both circular sawing and planing facilities I usually buy my timber sawn and then plane it up. However, more timber than ever is now reaching the racks in a planed and ready-to-use state. You will almost certainly be able to find timber labelled as Planed All Round (PAR) or Planed Square Edged (PSE). However, there are a number of hand-held electric power planes (see *below*) that will make light work of planing timber and it's well worth considering buying one of these. I always check my timber very carefully before starting work and mark in my face side, face edge marks (see page 99). If you don't start with carefully selected and prepared timber you can't hope to get a good finish at the end.

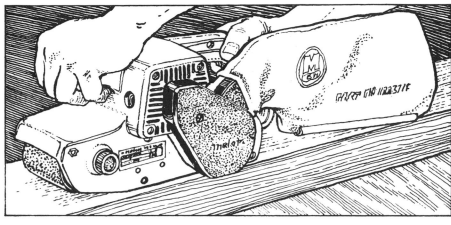

The range of surform planes available make easy work of shaping up timber. There are a whole family of surform tools and they all cut wood with small serrated teeth. Skewing the tool (by about 30°) as you use it allows you to remove shavings more rapidly than if you just work it backwards and forwards.

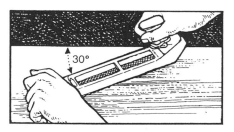

Spokeshaves (*below* and *right*) are invaluable for many wood-shaping jobs, especially finishing off curves. They are available with either convex or concave soles.

A belt sander (*above*) is the ideal tool for evening up boards that have been glued together. It is a powerful machine and its weight rapidly removes wood so do keep it moving as you use it or it will create hollows. You can buy an attachment called a skirt or shoe that fits onto the bottom of the tool and keeps it 'floating' on the surface thus preventing unevenness. The dust bag should be emptied frequently. Keep an eye on the belt to make sure that it stays in the middle; a tracking device should keep it running centrally. Different grades of grit are available so once the initial sanding has been done, change the belt to a finer grit for finishing off.

Recently I used an electric palm sander (*above*) for the first time which is a great boon for working on small surfaces or around small battens. I used the palm sander while working on the screen (page 13) and was very pleased at the speed, lightness and manoeuvrability of this tool.

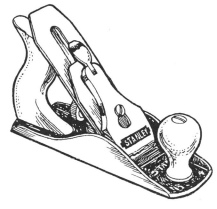

A smoothing plane is one of the best tools for finishing off work, but do re-sharpen the blade regularly. You can buy a special jig to hold the blade at the correct angle for this which is wonderfully easy to use. Once the blade is razor sharp, take it out of the jig and place it flat on the oilstone. Rub it across the oilstone a few times to remove the burr on the back. Since the smoothing plane is a finishing-off tool I round off the corners on the oilstone too to stop the edges from digging in. Set the cap iron abut 3mm (⅛in) back from the top of the blade. A piece of candle wax rubbed onto the sole will make certain of a magnificent finish to your work.

Glasspaper is very useful for finishing off but don't use it just as it is in your fingers as you will create an uneven surface. Wrap it round a cork block or piece of waste wood.

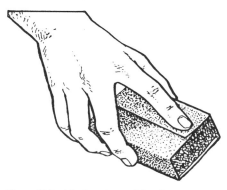

You will find that a piece of furniture progresses quite quickly through the initial stages of marking out, cutting joints etc, but it is the finishing process that takes the time. Be prepared to spend many hours in getting this right before you apply any stains, varnishes, or polish.

Publications and Catalogues

There is a wealth of published information available on woodworking, tools, etc. to help you enjoy your hobby. The following list is not exhaustive but the literature gained from it will give you an excellent perspective of what tools are available.

Practical Woodworking Published monthly and available from newsagents. Includes articles on how to work with wood, projects, new tools, suppliers, and so on – a must for the aspiring woodworker!

The Swedish Finnish Timber Council 21/25 Carolgate, Retford, Notts DN22 6BZ. Send large S.A.E. for free DIY leaflets on a whole range of projects.

Craft Supplies Ltd Specialise in wood turning and a full range of fittings, finishes, etc. Their fascinating catalogue reads like a book! Price: £2.00 including p. & p. from The Mill, Millers Dale, Buxton, Derbyshire SK17 8SN.

Record Marples Ltd The full catalogue of tools from this world-renowned toolmaker is a must for the keen woodworker. Send large S.A.E. to Record Marples Ltd, Parkway Works, Sheffield S9 3BL.

Stanley Tools A huge catalogue full of tools, chisels, tapes, screwdrivers etc. and 'How to' leaflets. Send large S.A.E. to The Stanley Works Ltd, Woodside, Sheffield S3 9PD.

Makita Electric (UK) Ltd Produce a range of quality power tools. Send a large S.A.E. for their *Power-Craft* brochure to Makita Electric (UK) Ltd, 8 Finway, Dallow Road, Luton, Beds LU1 1TR.

Black & Decker As well as producing probably the largest catalogue of tools for home and garden available, Black & Decker also have a professional tools department. Send large S.A.E. to Black & Decker Ltd, Westpoint, The Grove, Slough, Berks SL1 1QQ.

Emmerich (Berlon) Ltd This company produces workbenches in a variety of sizes. Send a large S.A.E. for information to: Emmerich (Berlon) Ltd, Wotton Road, Ashford, Kent TN23 2JY.

Notes on the Sponsors of this book

Stanley Tools, The Stanley Works Ltd, Woodside, Sheffield S3 9PD

Innovative design and continual high standards of manufacture have made Stanley Tools one of the leading manufacturers of hand tools. Stanley's product range has grown to over 1,400 top quality lines including well-known trademarks such as 'Bailey' planes, 'Powerlock' rules, 'Steelmaster' hammers, 'Yankee' spiral ratchet screwdrivers, 'Surform' shaver tools, 'Horizon' levels, 'Mole' gripping pliers, and of course, the ever popular 'Stanley' knife itself.

The comprehensive range of tools available are geared to the needs of both the professional and the DIY user. All Stanley products share the same attention to detail that ensures a job is well done, and around 300 have been accepted by the Design Council Index as examples of the best in British design. The most recent of these is the range of four Interlock trimming knives which have an innovative wedge locking action to hold the blade securely whilst in use.

Stanley have always been leaders in design and technology, and recently the company has been at the forefront of the development of ultrasonic measuring equipment with the launch of their dual mode Estimator.

A Yankee repair service and free leaflets on tools and woodworking techniques are some of the other services that this company provides.

Makita Electric (UK) Ltd, 8 Finway, Dallow Road, Luton, Beds LU1 1TR

Makita have now developed a complete range of hand-held power tools for the discerning craftsman – the *Power-Craft* range. The range includes: a jigsaw with variable speed and lots of power; a finishing sander with orbital action; a palm sander which is quite beautiful to use and extremely versatile; and a powerful belt sander with a shoe or 'skirt' to help you achieve a completely flat surface.

The circular saw comes complete with a tungsten carbide blade as standard and cuts wood smoothly without vibration. For the accurate cutting of angles, or indeed cross cutting, the mitre saw is excellent. It is fully guarded and the motor is equipped with an electric brake to protect the operator. The power planer is capable of planing up the roughest sawn timber. It is also able to cut rebates, and has a groove in the sole plate to allow the cutting of 45° angles.

There are two drills, a variable speed hammer drill and a smaller rotary drill both of which have belt clips. One of the most useful accessories for these drills is the vertical drill stand to ensure accurate drilling at 90°. In addition there are two battery-powered drills which come complete with chargers. The variable speed cordless screwdriver drill even has a built-in spirit level on the top.

Completing the range is a well-designed plunge router. This machine is capable of the most delicate cuts and yet has sufficient power to cut out stair strings. Safety features include an on/off switch in the handle, the plunge action at finger-tip control, a perspex shield to protect the operator from flying splinters and a three-turret head for quick adjustment.

AEG (UK) Ltd, 217 Bath Road, Slough, Berks SL1 4AW

This major company produces a universal woodworking machine that is ideal for dedicated hobbyist woodworkers and smaller professional craftsmen who have limited space for the machines they need, yet still aim for high-quality work.

The *Maxi* is compact (overall area just over 1 m²) and light enough to be moved easily into a corner on its castors when not in use, yet it performs full sawing, thicknessing, tenoning, morticing, planing and moulding operations. Its cast-iron table gives all-important rigidity and it can carry out really precise sawing – cutting, edging, mitre cutting and panel cutting, both straight and with an inclining saw blade giving an angle of up to 45°. It has a depth of cut of up to 90mm and a thicknessing range of up to 150mm. The automatic feed and central guidance ensures accuracy.

The *Maxi* has facilities for tenoning and deep morticing; in deep morticing the single 'joystick-style' lever gives considerable control and the machine has positive lateral and depth stops. For tenoning the retracting carriage is bearing-mounted and the adjustable fence has a 0–45° range so that cutting is not only straightforward but precise.

To cope with the demands likely to be made upon it, the six-function machine has a 1.5kw (2HP) motor and a lockable main on-off switch for continuous working. This can be over-ridden by 2 emergency stop buttons situated in easy reach. All moving parts are guarded for safety.

Sadolin (UK) Ltd, Sadolin House, Meadow Lane, St Ives, Cambridgeshire PE17 4UY

This firm produces a complete range of microporous wood protection products. *Superdec* gives a dense opaque finish. Available in a number of colours, it is said to prevent blistering or peeling. Furthermore, it can be applied to previously painted or stained softwood, hardwood, plywood or new timber in the house or garden.

Joinery-protecting *Extra* comes in a selection of light fast colours. It provides a higher build finish on exterior joinery when optimum water repellency and dimensional stability are required. Combining resins and natural pigments, the manufacturer claims it provides an extremely durable semi-gloss, translucent finish for timber. Maintenance normally involves cleaning the surface with water and a stiff brush and reapplying one coat of *Extra*.

Sadolin *Holdex*, a lacquer for interior timbers, is now offered in a new high-gloss finish. It forms a strong surface film that is highly resistant to water and alcohol. The lacquer allows for movement and will not 'yellow'.

Classic decorative wood protection enhances the natural beauty of timber while providing lasting protection against blue stain and mould growth. It can be used on interior and exterior new softwood, hardwood, plywood, blockboard and particle board. It can also be applied to planed or rough sawn timber.

Kronospan UK Ltd, Chirk, Wrexham, Clwyd LL14 5NT

Kronospan produce *Keyboard* which is a melamine-faced board suitable for the chest on page 19, the table on page 57 and the freestanding shelves on page 31.

The *Keyboard* panels are made from 15mm (⅝in) thickness chipboard that is pressed and edged with melamine surface papers. The melamine provides a durable finish that is easy to clean. There is a wide range of colours and wood effects – white, beige, grey, teak, mahogany, light oak and black ash. Sizes available are predominantly 2440mm (8ft) length with widths in 75mm (3in) increments from 152mm (6in) to 610mm (24in).

Keyboard is available from most major DIY stores as are a wide range of fixings and various project books that give ideas on design and step-by-step instructions.

European Industrial Services Ltd (manufacturers of Nettlefolds screws), Woden Road West, King's Hill, Wednesbury, West Midlands WS10 7TT

Nettlefolds *Supascrews* have a number of advantages over conventional woodscrews. First, they will fasten in virtually any material – hardwood, softwood, chipboard and even thin sheet steel. Secondly, the head is as hard as the tip of the screwdriver making them abuse-proof. Not only does this make inserting the screws easier, but they can also be taken out without having to struggle with a deformed head. The recess in the head, which is in the shape of a cross, has been improved to give the screws 'stick fit'. This means that the screwdriver clings to the screw making them easy to install one-handed in awkward corners.

To speed up installation, two features have been incorporated – a sharp point and deep, sharp threads. The sharp point penetrates the surface at once, does not slip across it and makes getting started easy. The thread form is more widely spaced, deeper and sharper than on a conventional woodscrew with a parallel, not tapered, shank which helps reduce any tendency to split the wood when working close to end grain. The screws are case-hardened which ensures that they are not weakened by being narrower.

Nettlefolds also produce *Multis* – a new type of screw which comes in black, white, red, blue, gold and brown to co-ordinate or contrast with different shades of wood, man-made boards and laminate finishes. The colour is plated so that it will not chip or flake. These hardened steel screws can be used in wood and man-made boards.

The head has a Simons drive recess which is less obtrusive than the slot on a conventional screw. A Simons screwdriver bit is available for use with *Multis* which fits neatly into a power driver or hand-held driver. One size bit fits the complete range of sizes.